### The Nine Day Novel series bonuses include:
- ✓ Four Part Story Structure Scrivener Starter File
- ✓ Four Part Story Structure MS Word Starter File
- ✓ FREE and Bargain Book Marketing Submission Site List
- ✓ *Nine Day Novel: Self-Editing* Bonus Videos
- ✓ And much more!

### *Two ways to get instant access to the bonuses*

**ONE -** Enter your email on any of our free product pages at https://authorbasics.com/shop/ and click the "Download Now" button.

**TWO** - Avoid entering your email for each freebie you want by becoming a FREE member of Author Basics, our author training community, at https://authorbasics.com/join/
**THEN** Login at https://authorbasics.com/my-account/
**VISIT** https://authorbasics.com/bonus-content/ or https://authorbasics.com/shop/
**ENJOY** the freebies!

## ::Disclaimer

This book is for informational purposes only. The author makes no claims or warranties to the accuracy of the contents. The information found within the contents of this book may contain third-party products and services. These third-party materials consist of products and opinions expressed by their owners. As such, the author and/or the publisher do not assume responsibility or liability for any third-party material or opinions expressed.

The use of recommended third-party material does not guarantee any success and/or earnings related to you or your business. Publication of such third-party material is simply a recommendation and an expression of the author's own opinion of that particular material.

Links to third-party resources may be affiliate links, meaning the author may receive compensation if a service is ultimately purchased from such a link.

NINE DAY NOVEL
# SELF
# PUBLISHING

## STEVE WINDSOR

Published by

Vixen

# VIXEN ink

Although the author and publisher have made every effort to ensure that the information in this book was correct at press time, the author and publisher do not assume and hereby disclaim any liability to any party for any loss, damage, or disruption caused by errors or omissions, whether such errors or omissions result from negligence, accident, or any other cause.

## *NINE DAY NOVEL: SELF-PUBLISHING*

A VIXEN ink book/Published by arrangement with the author

Copyright © 2015 by Steve Windsor

All rights reserved.

No part of this book may be reproduced, scanned, or distributed in any printed or electronic form without permission

(Printed Version)
ISBN-13: 978-1522761396
ISBN-10: 152276139X

## Dedication

*To you . . . becoming a "published" author.*

# TABLE OF CONTENTS

# NINE DAY NOVEL: SELF-PUBLISHING YOUR NOVEL TO KINDLE AND CREATESPACE

# INTRODUCTION

## CONGRATULATIONS

You did it! You finally finished that work of fiction you've always wanted to write. You've outlined, written, and edited your novel. Now what?

If you're like me, once I was done writing and editing, there I was with my beautiful manuscript, and no clue what to do next.

But this is your moment and you can finally call yourself an author. After all, what's an author but a person who's written an entire book . . . start to finish. That's an author, isn't it?

But are you yet? A *published* author, that is? And how *does* an independent author publish, anyway?

Until you can afford a printing press to print copies as you need them, or you create an email list that allows you to make a living selling directly to your adoring fans, you're going to need a company/service to perform all of the delivery logistics for you.

## The 800 pound gorilla

Your book needs to be available to as many potential readers as it can be in the least amount of hassle/time that it takes to do that. Until the other on-line retailers figure out how to dethrone them, that's Amazon.

NOTE: I'm not saying it isn't worth having your books available anywhere and everywhere you can—Kobo, iBooks, Barnes and Noble, Smashwords, et al.—just that from an opportunity cost standpoint, the biggest bang for your book's buck and the best use of your time is. . . Amazon—KDP and CreateSpace.

But by now you're worn out.

In *Nine Day Novel: Authorphobia*, we overcame the fear that you'd suck at writing. In *NDN: Outlining* and *Writing*, I hammered you with Four Part Story Structure enough to make Larry Brooks proud. And in *NDN: Self-Editing*, you were introduced to one of the often overlooked parts of publishing fiction—using Scrivener to clean up your draft.

I threw in some of the basics of writing fiction dialogue into that book—learning action beats, exposition, dialogue, and sentence structure, just to keep things interesting.

Yet, as if finishing your novel could be any more anticlimactic, as far as the millions of readers out in reader-land goes, none of them can even purchase your book . . . yet.

**Don't be afraid. Have a stiff drink.**

Without getting too in-depth and preachy about this, your first novel's job is to suck, your second one's job is to suck less, your third's is to be okay, your fourth's is to be decent, your fifth's is to be good, your sixth's is to better, your eighth's is to be better still, your ninth's is to be better than that.

Provided you haven't starved to death, drank yourself into an Ernest Hemingway or F. Scott Fitzgerald stupor, or hurled your exhausted carcass off the nearest skyscraper —your tenth book should make you some money. (Yes, I left number seven out. Lucky seven. . . That could be the money maker, baby!)

It's not quite as bad as all that, but you get the gist of what I'm saying. Practice and perseverance.

I know you have kids, a job, and a micromanaging boss, but once again, the answer is? . . . Darth Vader hard work!

**THIS IS A HOW-TO BOOK**

If you've read any of the other books in this *Nine Day*

*Novel* series, you know that I like to get down to business and talk about the reality of writing and being an author in the new self-publishing world. Put the "how" back in how-to.

**Figure out what works for you**

I'll say it again—there's no system. What works for one author in a genre may or may not work for another in a different one.

Information, tactics, strategies, hard work, practice, and experimentation is what will work for you. Self-publishing's no different from any other endeavor—the harder you work, the more successful you'll be.

Your strategy will depend on the amount of time you have to spend on the self-publishing process and how hard you're willing to work to succeed at learning the systems that have been invented to make all this "easier."

Barring independent wealth that allows you to outsource all of it and simply function as a publisher, at this point in the process, you'll need to learn technology and systems, and develop skills that have nothing to do with being a great writer.

**WHAT'S AN AUTHORPRENEUR?**

There's a cute new term that's emerged amidst all this "self"-everything as it relates to aspiring authors. That term is supposed to encompass the fact that even as you learn to write decent > well > good > great, you'll need to familiarize yourself with the software, technology, marketing, finance, and other business tools and skills necessary to publish, promote, and otherwise pimp out your books.

Twenty percent of success will be writing good books and eighty percent will be applying best business practices, email list building, learning self-publishing systems and rinse-and-repeat book marketing strategies that require hard work to win.

I'm here to help you learn all those.

## MY WRITER VOICE

That last section is as good a time as any to (re)introduce you to my writer "voice."

In *Nine Day Novel: Authorphobia, Outlining, Writing and Self-editing*, I talked about some hardcore "methods" that I use to pump words onto the page. Now we're going to get down and dirty with what has to be done to get those words pretty, published, printed, and pimping hard on the street corner, making you some "mun-nay!"

(WARNING: If an analogy to fictitious street corner hookers offends your delicate sensibilities, you're in the wrong book.)

But if you're like me, and you don't have extra time to play nice-nice and fool around being PC, well, young Jedi, you've come to the right place—hard work and no frills central.

## Darth Vader?

It's in that spirit of raw, hard work that this book series has taken shape as a "Darth Vader"-style kick in the pants to my fellow writer peeps. I love other authors who are struggling with wading through the often daunting task of overcoming their fears so they can outline, write, edit, self-publish, and market their first novel.

Why? Because I was you and when I was, I wish someone had boiled this stuff down to actionable chunks for me. So that's what I'm trying to do for you.

And as your wicked wake up call, occasionally in these books, I beat on you a little bit to suck it up and get down and dirty with the "distasteful" hard work. So forgive me if my style offends you, but my "voice" isn't for everyone.

Enough said.

## THE "WISK" SECTION

It can be said by more than people than my wife, that too much of my aforementioned "voice" can grind on your nerves. That is true. It's also true that you can get happy joy-joy mushery in a million other books that'll tell you how you can succeed in seven minutes with no hard work.

For that reason, and because I'd read enough quotes of the master Stephen King's words of wisdom, I created my own quote section for my own books.

At the beginning of most chapters, you'll get a completely new, and if I'm honest about it, sarcastic and semi-naughty little tidbit from yours truly.

**WISK**—The "When I'm Stephen King" section. (Wait, was that my hypocrite meter pegging?)

## IT'S NOT EASY

"The only easy day . . . was yesterday"

I love the Navy SEALS for that.

I make no qualms in showing you that the task of writing and self-publishing a novel isn't the magic that many make it out to be. Yet it's also not the "easy path to a six-figure luxury lifestyle" that some claim it to be, either.

Yes, writing is enjoyable, entertaining, and empowering, but it's also more skill building, stubbornness, and suffering than any other job you'll love.

Study hard, learn hard, write hard. Dedicate yourself and do the hard work. That's what writing requires of you. Skill —relentless hard work and practice—trumps talent . . . every time.

## THE REAL "SYSTEM"

I told you earlier that there is no system—no one size fits all secret method. However, true systems are processes and procedures that you can perform over and over again. They improve and speed up the task each time. Systems, in their true form, help you win by increasing your efficiency at doing the hard work necessary to succeed.

But all too often systems are put forth as hidden magic formulas that are only available by paying someone else $97, $197, $497, or $997 to be let in on the secret. But let me assure you, once you look behind the curtain in the "Emerald City," guess what's back there? More hard work —Dorothy's gotta kill the wicked witch to get the red slippers back.

Dammit! I was afraid that was the answer. Next!

## HAVE SOME FUN

Writing and learning to write should be fun.

The subject of writing and self-publishing can get dry, sometimes even a little cheesy. As you can tell by now, I like to hose it down every once in a while with my own "observations."

My hope is that a little tongue-in-cheek humor is just the "whine" to go along with all that cheese.

# BOOK BONUSES

I wanted to make the *Nine Day Novel* series bonuses as valuable, if not more valuable, than the books themselves. So I've packed in things like a Four Part Story Structure Scrivener starter file, self-editing tutorial videos, and more.

For this book, the bonus is going to be BONUS VIDEOS to help you **successfully use Mailchimp and explain Scrivener's compile function for KDP and Create-Space**.

:: ACTION ITEM

**If you haven't already, you can get instant access to them by signing up for a free membership at:**

**https://authorbasics.com/join**

**And then logging in and accessing the video bonuses at:**

**https://authorbasics.com/ndn-sp-bv**

And there are many more bonuses at Author Basics.

# SCRIVENER

**WISK**

"Scrivener vs. Word—a $1000 massage vs. a hammer smashing your thumb." — Steve Windsor

**TIME TO LEARN SCRIVENER**

Scrivener is by far the most valuable and least expensive "Swiss Army knife" of self-publishing that you'll ever be afraid to buy and learn. Sadly, most new authors are simply scared to death of it for no good reason.

But, if you want:

- Easier outlining
- Drag and drop chapters, text, and sections
- Professional formatting control
- Easier chapters, documents, headings, and lists
- Friendly Table of Contents creation
- Image insertion and rendering
- Professional production of .pdf, .mobi, .epub files and more
- Power publishing to Kindle and CreateSpace

- And in general, management, maintenance, and back-up of all the physical files and formats that a small publishing house had to hire a team of six to do just ten years ago. . .

**If you want to get serious, it's time to learn Scrivener!**

Sure you can outsource all the production aspects of your book, but all that outsourcing is going to eat into your pocketbook and cause your launch costs to skyrocket beyond what your early books will be able to recover in revenues.

Sound like a business class? Authorpreneur, remember?

What I'm trying to say is that if I had to go back and outline, write, edit, format, compile, and publish 12 books in less than a year, to multiple formats on multiple platforms, *and* keep track of all the different versions of front matter, back matter, and the internals of multiple books in the same file . . . and share those files with my editors. . .? Yeah, I would've been overwhelmed long ago.

So let's put this one to bed. <u>Buy and learn Scrivener</u>. You can get your copy here: <u>https://authorbasics.com/z6qi/</u>

Last time I'll say it. Promise. Well, in this book, anyway. . .

## OKAY, YOU CAN USE WORD

Okay, if all you have is Word, then by all means write, but it will get complicated, scrolling up and down, trying to figure out where everything is, much less rearranging chapters, sharing files, formatting, converting files to .mobi. . . You get my drift.

**Here's a small jumpstart for all you Word holdouts.**

To help you get productive on day one, I've created a Four Part Story Structure Word .doc as a little bonus starter file to save you a little bit of time. Get it at:

https://authorbasics.com/4pss-word

## VERSUS GOOGLE DOCS

I like Google docs for sharing short documents online. I also charge clients money to convert their large Google doc or Word drafts into a .mobi file for KDP or .pdf file for CreateSpace. And the first thing I do in that process is import all that text into . . . Scrivener.

If it's already there, formatting costs less.

## FOR EDITING

In the "old" days, the only editors Lise and I could find on elance.com and Upwork were Word "track changes" people. And to work with them we'd have to export from Scrivener to a .doc file, let them make changes, accept their tracked changes in Word, then cut and paste those changes back into Scrivener, and then reformat every-thing. It was painful.

Now we share our Scrivener files directly with our editors via Dropbox and they edit right inside our master files. We've shaved days off of the editing timeline doing this.

Most of the functionality of Word's track changes features can be replaced when editing inside Scrivener. If you become a free member of Author Basics at: https://author-basics.com/join/ , the *NDN:Self-editing* bonus content post has videos on how I do that at:

https://authorbasics.com/self-editing-bonus-videos/

There are Scrivener basics videos on that post, as well.

# AMAZON

## WISK

"Amazon is like a big, hairy out of control 800 pound gorilla. You have to love him, but eventually you'll need to take away his bananas." — Steve Windsor

## AMAZON IS YOUR BOSS

We'll talk about the other online retailers in a more advanced book. For now, as a new author, you need to learn all about and get in love with Amazon. For all intents and purposes, in the beginning, Amazon's your "boss."

Every one of your readers is basically your boss as well, but Amazon writes your checks. I hesitate to use capitalistic lingo and call readers "customers," but that's exactly what they are. Your job is to turn them into repeat customers.

Yet in this, you and Amazon are at slight odds with each other. Amazon provides you a sales and delivery platform to sell your books and in return, you bring them new customers that they can sell other goods to directly. Make no mistake, that's the relationship.

You as an author know absolutely nothing about the people who buy your books from Amazon, save for the occasional review. **So your top priority is to get your readers off of Amazon and onto your author platform. More specifically, your email list.**

## AMAZON IS NOT A BOOKSELLER

What?

Amazon's the second largest online search engine, bowing only to Google.

As a search engine, readers find your books on Amazon by searching titles, keywords, author names, genres, and any other information that they think will help them solve their problems.

What are fiction readers' "problems" anyway? Boredom and belonging. Pure and simple. And as it happens, as a fiction author, you can cure both of those problems . . . for money. But if you have to keep repeating the process of finding new readers every month, you'll wear yourself out before you make any headway.

## GET YOUR READERS OFF AMAZON

Readers love to be entertained and they love access—

being on the inside.

You have the solution to both of those problems.

Your book should entertain at the very least. But believe me, it doesn't have to be Tolstoy to do that. Good, not god-like, is what you're going for.

The second issue of access and belonging helps both you and your reader solve your problems together. You need loyal fans—repeat customers—and they need insider access and community and connection with you.

This is where your email list and a freebie comes in. That'll get some of your readers off of Amazon and onto your list, so you can speak to them directly.

Write a short story, novella, guide to the world of your novels . . . **anything that a reader would find interesting, and then offer it for free as an incentive to them for signing up to your email author updates list.**

How do I do that?

First, let's talk about your author platform.

# YOUR AUTHOR "PLATFORM"

## WISK

"Jack Daniels and a long weekend. That's what it takes."
— Steve Windsor

## YOUR AUTHOR WEBSITE

First, let's define what your author platform is, because the opinions and definitions are all over the map. Your platform consists of all the methods, mechanisms, and marketing that you use to connect with your potential readers and eventual fans. Here are some of the examples:

### Website

Your author website will be the primary way that your readers connect directly with you. It's the hub of your author platform, and it only has one job—gather email addresses from visitors to convert them into paying customers—readers.

### Domain Name

The first thing you need is to pick a domain name. You can't have a website without it. (Well, you can, but we'll talk about that later) The simplest, easiest, and fastest way to solve this problem is to use your own name. Your work may change; your name won't.

Only use a .com as they get the most traffic and most of the general public—readers—still don't understand domains like .li (Lichtenstein) or .tv (Tuvelo).

If you have a common name and your domain name is taken, then use something like janedoeauthor.com or janedoenovels.com or janedoewrites.com

**Naming Tools**

If you want to brainstorm domain names other than your given name, namestation.com is a great tool, as is Shopify's tool to search for variations of keywords.

**Registrars**

You can buy your domain name from a domain name registrar. I use namecheap.com now, and have used www.iwantmyname.com.

**Website Hosting**

Your domain name is your website's address. This points

to the actual files that make up your website. Your website files live on a web host's computers somewhere in a datacenter in the cloud (the internet).

I've hosted my many websites on 1&1, Hostgator, VPN, GoDaddy, BlueHost, and on webfaction. The easiest to navigate and maintain are <u>BlueHost</u> and Hostgator.

As a newbie author, you need easy. That's <u>BlueHost</u> or Hostgator.

**Wordpress**

Wordpress is *the* content management system that runs millions of websites on the Internet. Wordpress makes tasks like page, post, and forms creation much easier. Trust me, your easy option for running your own website is Wordpress.

Many web hosts have a packaged Wordpress install in which you can click one button and it'll be installed for you. Hostgator and BlueHost both have this feature.

**Wordpress Themes**

A theme is a template that determines how your Wordpress website will look and feel to an end user. There are simply millions of them—paid and free—to choose from. Luckily, Wordpress comes with some great built-in themes now that you can use to get started.

Start looking for premium themes at Themeforest.com.

## Pages and Posts

Wordpress started out as a blog platform but has since become a dynasty. Yet it's still built around two major components—pages and posts. Pages are static pieces of content that don't change. Posts are what everyone understands as blogging. They're time based releases of information and usually written about subjects related to the website.

**The minimum pages you need on your website:**

## Homepage

What this site is about—what it can do for the visitor. (Remember, boredom cure.) You'll want your email opt-in form, your author photo, a little blurb about you, your latest book—if you've written it yet—if not you need to go write that promo piece we talked about, because that's the core of your email opt-in offer. Also, your latest blog posts. And in the footer of every page you'll want links to follow you on social media—Facebook, Twitter. . .

## About Page

This is who I am and this is what I do and this is why I do it. Use the word "you" (your reader) more than you use the word "I." Your readers are there to connect with you, but that's all about *them*.

Include an email opt-in form on the sidebar and your author image on the page as well.

**Books Page**

These are the books I've written. Covers are the perfect image here as they are the coolest to look at . . . hopefully. Links to each individual book page (you'll need to create a page for each book), title, short description, link to your Amazon buy page. Review blurbs if you've got them yet, and as always an email opt-in box to subscribe to your list.

If you haven't written your book yet, create the page anyway and use as much info as you have about it—title, demo cover, summary. . .

**Contact**

This is how you can contact me. Most Wordpress themes have a built-in email form that people can use to submit a question and have it emailed directly from your site. At minimum this page should tell your reader how to get in touch with you. Email address, Facebook page, Twitter handle. . . And can you guess by now? Email opt-in form.

Most new authors can get away with just those pages, because what you really need is a finished freebie and your first book. And as long as you have links to put inside your book that point people to sign up to your list, your website is functional.

## Blog Posts

Blogging has become debatably a difficult way to draw in traffic to your website. The blog-o-sphere is jammed with content, and blogging is writing, so I'd prioritize writing your freebie and your first book over blogging. Regardless, if you do write blog posts, make sure your blog post page has an email opt-in form in the sidebar and every single post page does as well.

## Wordpress Plugins

Plugins add functionality to your Wordpress website. They're little applications that integrate with Wordpress to do things that it doesn't.

The plugins I use the most are:
- <u>Pretty Links</u>—a redirector so you can put a link to your book's Amazon page inside your book internals before you publish and find out that link. Otherwise, once you publish to

Amazon and receive your book's ASIN and link to your book sales page on Amazon, you'll have to fix that inside your book's internals file, compile it again, and republish your .mobi file. It's painful.

- <u>UpdraftPlus Backup/Restore</u>—Back up all of your Wordpress files. Trust me. . .
- <u>MailChimp's email opt-in form</u>—I get fancier with this, but this is the minimum functionality you'll need.
- Alternatively <u>Aweber's email opt-in form</u>

Let's recap. That was a little less than a thousand words designed to get one point across to you—your website's job is to gather visitor emails to go on your email marketing list. Not be pretty, or cool, or fun—get emails!

## BONUSES

As I mentioned before, the way to get reader emails is to give them something worth handing over their email for.

In fiction, this is a novella, short story, or "the world of" your series piece. This will be your bonus freebie, giveaway, enticer. . . Whatever you want to call it. And it's as "easy" as this.

**Write the piece.**

Take care as this is the first impression your reader may have of you, so don't just pump it out as fast as you can. It's as important as your novels are, more so.

**Compile the file.**

I prefer to use Scrivener to create a .pdf because most people have some sort of .pdf viewer. Some authors go so far as to ZIP a .pdf, .mobi and .epub file and provide that. For starters, use a .pdf.

**Upload and host the file.**

Dropbox is free for the first five Gigs, so is Google drive. You can host on S3, but it costs. The reason for hosting is that direct downloads will tax your webserver and may crash it if you get too many at once.

**Get the shared link.**

In Dropbox, you can right click the file and get the sharing URL (address) of your file to put inside your email list's signup form—via Mailchimp or Aweber. Same thing in Google docs or S3—get the share link.

And that's the best point for us to break and talk about email list building services.

# EMAIL AUTORESPONDERS

## MAILCHIMP AND AWEBER

At their most basic level, email marketing software services store your subscribers' email addresses, send emails to them on your behalf when you set that up, and maintain statistics about your clicks and the open rates of email campaigns you send.

**Mailchimp and Aweber are the two largest email marketing software services for new authors.** The reason is that they are the most popular, least expensive, and "easiest" to use.

Many authors, myself included, have switched back and forth between each of them and they compete tooth and nail with each other for the bulk of the entry-level to intermediate market share of email marketing software providers.

The next step up from Mailchimp and Aweber is to upgrade to Infusionsoft.

**Forget I said, "Infusionsoft!"**

If you're a new author with no budget, you can't afford them. And if you have minimal to moderate technical abilities, Lynchburg, Tennessee will be on your speed dial. (It's where they make Jack Daniels Whiskey.)

All my lists are on Mailchimp right now, because I didn't like Aweber's forms and Aweber charges right away, while Mailchimp waits until you have 2,000 subscribers . . . unless, of course, you want some advanced features, then you gotta pay Mailchimp, too.

Neither are that expensive, averaging around $19/month in fees to start. So Ford-Chevy, Coke-Pepsi. . . This decision will be yours to live with, because no matter what people have told you about how "easy" it is . . . setting up email autoresponders ain't easy.

**A couple of the main differences**

**Aweber allows you to turn off double opt-in and Mailchimp doesn't.** You can do it with Mailchimp, but you need a plugin, a fifth of Jack Daniels, and a weekend. I'll tell you why this is important in a minute.

**Aweber's forms are "old"-looking and Mailchimp's are plain ugly . . . IMO.** And neither provide a nice slick horizontal form that you can simply drop in place and have work right out of the box. I've worked on it and until I found a plugin called **Mailchimp for Wordpress**, I always ended up hand-coding the CSS to make it look pretty.

So, you'll get forms, but all those pretty and perfect email opt-in boxes you see on everyone else's websites. . . Those are custom applications you can buy, or Lead-pages (an email marketing forms application/service that integrates with Wordpress), or OptimizePress (a Word-press theme and/or application). Both of which you have to pay for. For now, let's keep it simple.

**Basic email setup and forms**

Get an account with Mailchimp or Aweber, create a list, then create an opt-in form for that list. Each service has great tutorials to get that done.

You can host that form on your site by cutting and pasting the HTML you're given for the form, once you're done building it, right into a sidebar widget on your website.

However, it's easier to use those Mailchimp or Aweber Wordpress plugins I told you about in the website section. They make integrating with your email marketing software provider pretty easy.

Did I just say "easy?"

I suggest you use those plugins, give them the login information to your Mailchimp or Aweber account, and let the plugin handle how the opt-in form looks. Otherwise, spend money on Leadpages or OptimizePress, because DIY HTML cut and paste is more technical. You can do it . . . but keep the Jack Daniels handy.

So there it is—use the plugins to paste a form into a widget sidebar on your Wordpress website and you're golden. Now, a visitor to your website can enter their name and email and click a button and they're on your list. Perfect.

**But wait. Why would someone give you their email address?**

Human beings are pretty simple—they give in anticipation of getting. Most of them anyway—nurses aside—and giving you an email address is not something that most people like to do . . . unless they get something back. That's where that freebie you wrote comes in.

**But how do we actually *deliver* the freebie?**

Glad you asked. First, here's the standard email double opt-in process that both Aweber and Mailchimp adhere to. There are reasons, and I'll explain them, but first. . .

- I visit your website and see your email opt-in form, because you put it right in front of me on the page and I can't miss it.

- For some unknown reason I decide to give you my email address and click submit.
- Up pops a page that says thank you, but we need to verify your submission. Please go to your email and verify.
- I go to my email, find the verification email, and click to verify myself.
- Up pops another page. Thank you for subscribing to blah blah author's updates. Do you want to go to our website or edit your account details. WT. . .? I was already at your website.
- A final welcome email shows up in my inbox.

This is called double opt-in email subscription verification and it's a PITA. But because of spammers and scammers that give false email addresses to get access to free stuff and clutter up legitimate email lists with junk email addresses, the email marketing service providers require it.

The fact is that the more bounces due to bad emails and junk emails a service provider sends, the worse their own spam rating is. This causes them to get into trouble with spam watchers and virus protectors, and causes their mails to be sent to spam folders in individuals' email inboxes. Very bad.

Regardless, the process is the equivalent of being at a Russian checkpoint during the cold war—Are you Gregor Panovich? Da? Are you sure you're *the* Gregor Panovich?

Uh . . . Da? Okay, welcome to the gulag—I mean, list.

And the first thing "Gregor" will want to know—what does being "on the list" get me?

So we have to give Gregor some reason to want to be on the list, because being on a list, to most people, feels . . . invasive. Not "TSA strip searched at a checkpoint" invasive, but . . . uncomfortable.

For that reason, we give Gregor something really valuable, that he really wants, to get him to agree to being on the list.

Back to how to deliver that value to Gregor. The easiest, cheapest way is to host it on Dropbox.

So, since we already hosted our freebie file and got our link to it in the last section, we're going to use it now.

In both Aweber and Mailchimp there's the option to send a "final" email to a subscriber, which brings the "touch" count to three or four to sign up for your list, depending on how you look at it. In that final email, we'll send our new subscriber a link to the freebie.

You have to do this by customizing the final welcome email in Mailchimp to include the link to where your freebie file is being hosted. Then once your subscriber gets that last email, they can click the link and download the file.

But just like the US Southern border, most subscribers are used to this continual questioning to get to where they want to go, but it's still a PITA. So if you want to turn off double opt-in on Aweber, they'll let you do that, but Mailchimp is more complicated.

**Still want to turn off Mailchimp double opt-in?**

I don't blame you, because if a subscriber can only get that freebie by clicking the link that you send them in email, that proves to me the email is legit, so why not skip those intermediate steps?

# AUTHOR PLATFORM CONTINUED

## WISK

"I'll be honest with you—blogging's a pain in the ass." — Steve Windsor

## TO BLOG OR NOT TO BLOG

The average blog post is 500-1000 words and it takes longer to research, outline, and type those 1,000 words than your 1,000 word/hour novel-writing pace, so it's gonna chew into your novel-writing time every day that you do it.

There are veterans who've given up on blogging in favor of other methods of gathering eyeballs to put on their list.

If you want to, blog away. Just make sure you provide value and/or entertainment as you do, remembering that the entire purpose is to get someone to opt-in to your list.

That being said, you need to have some way of providing value-add beyond your books in order for long-term readers to care about you, but you can do that in other ways.

# PODCASTING

Podcasting has become one of the most popular choices for authorities to spread their message far and wide.

A podcast is much like a recorded Internet radio show that can be consumed on the listener's time schedule. They can listen to it on their commute, while they work on other things around the house, or as background to surfing social media on their computer.

Because of that, it's becoming more popular than video because it doesn't require the full attention of the listener.

The goal here is to connect with your audience, so you could have a podcast that answers reader questions, details worlds from your books, or outlines your writing process and how you brainstorm your ideas. The sky's the limit on creativity and how you entertain/connect with readers.

One of the greatest examples I can think of for fan con-nection and loyalty through entertainment is the "fast becoming a powerhouse," AMC fan shows. Both *The Walking Dead* and *Breaking Bad* had their own fan shows right after each new episode.

A host, random fan/celebrities, and often a star from the show would come on and discuss the episode with the host and fans.

Names of those shows: *The Talking Dead* and *Talking Bad*. Frickin' brilliant!

## How-to Podcast Cliff Notes

Get a quality microphone. <u>Samson Meteor Mic USB Studio Microphone</u> is cheap and it works. If you want the entire setup—mic, pop filter, and headphones—you can get the <u>Samson SAMTR Meteor Mic With Pop Filter and Headphone Bundle</u>. The mic plugs into your laptop or computer USB and gives you pro quality sound above and beyond your ear plug headphones and built-in microphone.

## Use Audacity

Audacity is a free multi-track audio editor and recorder. You can download the app at <u>http://sourceforge.net/projects/audacity/</u>. Once you record your podcast to Audacity and get the .mp3—your audio recording—you can host the files on Amazon S3 or Sound Forge or similar cloud storage sites. But be careful hosting the files directly on your website, as bandwidth and reliability issues will plague you.

For an in-depth podcasting tutorial, search on <u>iTunes for Podcast Makers</u>.

Also, John Lee Dumas has a free podcaster course https://authorbasics.com/free-podcast-course/

There are other places to host your podcast, like stitcher.-com, but we're going for simplicity as you get going. And once again, the goal here is to engage the reader to become your fan and give you their email address.

## VIDEOS

I'm assuming you're no stranger to YouTube, but there are a couple other video hosting websites out there worth looking at.

### Vimeo

Vimeo is free unless you want to host multiple HD videos, but there's an even better option for video hosting that has a business marketing focus.

### Wistia

Wistia is not only a video host for your videos, but it also has features like inserting call to action (CTA) buttons or even your email signup form into a video timeline. Cool functionality, but it will take a more technical learning curve from you.

**So for now, if you want to vidcast as a way to build rapport with your audience, use YouTube.**

Best recording applications to do that:

- **Camtasia**—a powerful (read expensive), yet easy-to-use screen recorder. PC and MAC versions
- **Snagit**—(less expensive) Screen capture and real-time video capture. PC and MAC.
- **Ecamm plugin for Skype**—to record Skype interviews.
- **Screencast-O-Matic**—FREE and basic desktop screen recorder. PC and MAC. Even the upgrade is pretty inexpensive and it works as advertised. All the videos in the bonus section were created with SOM.

Most Wordpress themes allow you to embed the share URL for a YouTube video directly into a blog post, so this is an easy way to create a "blog" from your videos.

Videos further connect fans to you, because they put a face to your name and books.

**CREATE A FACEBOOK AUTHOR PAGE.**

**Create a Facebook Author Page.**

If there was only one social media service that I could invest my time and energy in, it would be Facebook. Chances are, if you're new to the author realm, you're not new to Facebook. Not only are there book fans all over it, but there are long established author how-to groups there as well.

Create a Facebook page and then give it a custom URL like, https://www.facebook.com/AuthorSteveWindsor

Make sure you put a link to this page on your website and on your "About the Author" page in the back matter of your book.

On your Facebook fan page, you're going to talk to your readers, like a real human being, about what it's like to be an author, what book you're working on, and post images like book cover mockups and photos from any author engagements you go to. Insider access, remember.

**TWITTER**

I still don't have a good handle on Twitter. . .

Get it? Okay, dry humor aside, some authors have amassed huge audiences on Twitter by tweeting about their books, throwing up timely quotes, and in general, and again, engaging and connecting on a human level.

I'm currently using my handle @penvenom, but may switch to my name for the branding reasons mentioned earlier in this book.

## GOODREADS

Goodreads is a community of rabid readers that used to be its own entity and has since been absorbed by the Borg—I mean Amazon.

Regardless, every book you publish on Amazon will automatically get a Goodreads listing and you'll want to set up an account over there if for no other reason than to claim your book records under your author profile.

I've run Goodreads giveaways and participated sporadically, so I'm not the best one to give advice on how well it helps sell books. However, the fans over there are serious and take their book reading seriously, so tread lightly.

# BUILDING YOUR BOOK

## WISK

"There's nothing like a nice package . . . to sell a book." — Steve Windsor

## WHAT YOUR BOOK IS

To readers, your book is a cover image, title, subtitle, description, and a bunch of reader reviews buried in a sea of other books on Amazon. To get it to float to the top of that churning ocean of obscurity like a big orange buoy in front of them, you need to do the following:

## WRITE A GOOD BOOK

This goes without saying, but I'm saying it anyway. A decent—not perfect, but good—book tells a compelling story about a protagonist's quest and struggle against an antagonistic force in order to ascend to a higher state of being.

It does this by following a set structure of setup, inciting event and run for your life, turn and face the danger and fight back and lose, and then eventually accept reality and fight back and win in a climax battle scene to ride into the sunset.

## CLEAN UP YOUR IMAGES

If you want to include images. . .

Photo images should be inserted into Scrivener in JPEG (or .jpeg) or PNG (.png) format at 300 dpi with center alignment (don't copy and paste them). The reason for the large resolution is that your printed CreateSpace book needs high resolution images for them to display nicely on a printed page.

For tables and drawings I pretty much use PNG as I don't like to mess with GIFs.

Careful with sizes, because KDP won't display anything over 5M correctly. Also, your ebook file size affects the royalty and pricing that you can choose. If your final file is less than three megabytes, you can select $0.99 to $200.00. If it's greater than or equal to three megabytes and less than 10 megabytes, $1.99 to $200.00. 10 megabytes or greater, $2.99 to $200.00. And that will affect whether you can use some of the free or $0.99 marketing launch strategies that are available.

Images inside ebooks are black art, because there are so many different devices rendering ebook files out there that it's tough to insert images that will display perfectly on all devices.

There are several discussions on image size on the internet, including Amazon's antiseptic instructions. Here are a couple I've found useful:

http://mademers.com/globalindieauthor/2014/04/significant-change-to-kindle-image-requirements/

https://kdp.amazon.com/community/thread.jspa?threadID=186238

And Amazon's. . .

https://kdp.amazon.com/help?topicId=A1B6GKJ79HC7AN

**Inserting Images in Scrivener**

Everything readable in Scrivener happens in a text document. So if you want to insert an image on a page of its own, make a new document, import the image file into the binder (outline side on the left) of Scrivener. Then place your cursor inside the document file where you want the image and drag the image from the binder to the document. Easier done than said, I guess.

Once you're done, you can double click the image to pull

up a scaling tool to make the image whatever percentage of its maximum size that you want.

**Oh, and a little known tip on how to link an image to a URL inside Scrivener:**

Place your cursor to the right or left of the image, hold down shift and press the right or left arrow on your keyboard to "select" the image—depending on what side of the image your cursor is on, of course. This highlights the image, though you may not be able to tell it's highlighted. Then go to the EDIT > ADD LINK menu item in Scrivener. Type in the link you want and voila. Be sure to test out the link by clicking on the image.

**Cover Image Sizes**

Here's a tutorial on Amazon's cover images guidelines.

https://kdp.amazon.com/help?topicId=A2J0TRG6OPX0VM

I make all my cover images as big as Amazon allows—2820x4500 pixels for best quality. And I import them into Scrivener's binder using the FILE > IMPORT > FILES. . . menu item.

**SPELLCHECK YOUR DRAFT**

After proofreading your entire file, manually use your spelling and grammar checker to sift through the entire file for errors.

There's a reason I put this suggestion in here, because no matter how good your editor is or how many times you've read your manuscript, you've missed something. I guarantee that.

## HIRE A PROFESSIONAL EDITOR

Readers no longer tolerate—if they ever did—constant grammatical, spelling, and sentence structure issues inside self-published books. Because the flip side of self-publishing being a mainstream and legitimate pathway to being considered a "published" author, is that you are now a professional in the eyes of your readers. And professionals don't make mistakes.

Oh, you'll be forgiven a few, but repeated errors in your novel will get you a naughty review and a smack on the back of the head. Trust me—the back of my head hurts. . .

## USE A PRETTY FONT

A quick note about fiction fonts.

Fonts are very subjective and designers are very passionate about their use. For good reason too, because they can change the mood and feel of your novel. A reader's perception of the professional nature of your book is also affected by font selection.

Fiction books are generally printed in serif fonts. Serif fonts are the ones with small decorative line added to the basic form of a character—the ones with the little spikes at the tips. I'll list some of the more popular, though this isn't a complete list.

- Adobe Garamond Pro
- Minion Pro
- Times New Roman
- Georgia
- Adobe Caslon Pro

The importance of fonts is that their look and feel supports the tone and theme of your story. Old world fonts support more formal storylines and "looser" serif fonts support a casual storyline. In addition, page count is affected by which fonts you choose.

I once shaved 25 pages off of the page count by switching the text to Minion Pro. I currently use Adobe Garamond Pro for *The Fallen* series because it feels more "old-world."

As a suggestion, start with Minion or Adobe Garamond Pro.

## Font Size

As for font size, fiction novels are generally printed from 11 to 13 point size. Any smaller and it will be difficult to read, and any larger and it tends not to look "right" to a seasoned book reader.

Much of our font discussion won't relate to Kindle publishing as most ebook readers convert just about everything they touch to Georgia font.

There have been efforts to embed more fonts into ebook readers, but they still render most book files into a default font.

## FORMAT LIKE A PRO

There are certain standard structures to formatting a fiction book. **At minimum, a fiction novel is structured as front matter, body of the book, and back matter.**

The front matter contains things like title page, copyright, and dedication. The back matter contains information about the author, more books a reader can buy, and a request for reviews. The body of the book is usually split into sections, chapters, and scenes.

Here are some rough rules about how the body of the

book internals are organized. As in everything, the rules are broken, but here's what they are.

## Sections

Sections are large portions of a story that are logically separated from other sections. They're much larger than chapters. For instance, if the first half of your book takes place 100 years in the past and the second half takes place in the "present," then you might want to separate those with clear section markers. John Sanford's *Buried Prey* is sectioned this way and titled "Then" and "Now."

I sectioned my *Fallen* series of novels literally at the breaks in the Four Part Story Structure and titled them as the theme of that section.

In Scrivener, sections are top-level folders that contain all the subfolders—chapters—for that section.

There's a way in Scrivener's compile function to force the Section title onto a right hand (recto) page for a print book's internals, because that's where it traditionally goes.

## Chapters

A chapter's job is to convey one main idea or sequence of events. Let's use my favorite: robbing a bank.

- The drive to the bank
- Jump out of the car
- Rush into the bank
- Shoot up the lobby
- Get the cash from the vault
- Rush outside to a barrage of police gunfire
- Wounded and bleeding get into the getaway car and
- Narrowly escape. . .

These are all scenes within the "Bank Robbery" chapter.

In Scrivener, chapters are sub-folders inside section folders. Chapter folders contain individual documents—scenes.

And that leads us to the next section.

**Scenes**

Scenes are sequences of events inside a chapter. The reason they're separated is to give the reader a grounded sense of where they are, or let them know that something significant inside a chapter has changed.

Think of a movie where the bank robbers are in the getaway car driving to the bank and then all of a sudden the movie cuts and they're inside the bank yelling at tellers. Those are two different scenes that are separated in a fiction novel by an empty line.

You create that empty line in Scrivener by making a new document inside a folder and placing an empty line between documents in the compile settings when you package—compile—your book's internals. (More on how to do that later.)

## Paragraphs

Paragraphs have long been a standard way to separate ideas. There are two main ways to separate paragraphs —indenting and placing spaces between them.

Normally, **non-fiction uses an empty line between paragraphs with no indent of the first line, and fiction has no space between paragraphs, but *does* indent the first line**. In fiction, the first word of the paragraph is usually indented around .25″, but this often comes down to personal choice.

NOTE: A common mistake new authors make is to use *both* paragraph separation methods at the same time— space between paragraphs *and* indented first lines. Don't.

You can control paragraph separation in Scrivener both inside the default text settings and inside the Compile function. You can override whatever settings you have as you type and edit, by changing the formatting inside the

Compile function. This is the preferred method as you have all the control to produce your various files inside the Compile function.

## Paragraph Alignment

In fiction, paragraph text is usually displayed with justified alignment—a smooth and aligned, not "ragged," right edge. Pick up any drugstore paperback novel and you'll see this.

This can also be controlled with Scrivener inside Compile's "Formatting" section.

## Page Breaks

In Scrivener, page breaks are inserted right before sections and chapters. They prevent the text from simply running together. They also provide a logical and graphical way for a reader to take a breath before diving back into the action.

Each document has a "Pg Break Before" check box in the Contents section of the Compile function that allows you to manually place a page break before any document you wish. Or you can automatically insert standard page breaks by altering the settings inside the Separators section in the Compile function.

I'll go over this in detail later, but here are some general hints.

Chapters are a good way to separate groups of characters within the same story. For instance, in *Game of Thrones,* the list of character arcs is huge. However, there are characters that travel together, or are in the same location or on the same arc. It's logical to start a new chapter when you switch from one set of characters to another.

You should also change chapters when you switch storylines, or character arcs, or move from points in the past versus the future versus the present, to help your reader orient themselves with in your story.

# FRONT MATTER BASICS

## WISK

"In books, as in dating, your front . . . matters." — Steve Windsor

## CREATING FRONT MATTER

Front matter is the beginning pages of a book and they convey a ton of information to readers. Front matter usually includes, at minimum, the Title Page, Copyright Page, and Dedication.

## BONUS GIVEAWAY PAGE

One of the best email marketing list builders—read that as highest converting—pages you can place in your book is a bonus offer page. Don't be shy about this, make it one of the first things a reader sees when they open your book.

Take a look at the one in this book as a guide, but it can be as simple as, "Hey, you can get the next book in the series for free by going to my website and signing up for free updates."

Nick Stephenson suggests a strategy of having a permafree novella available online and pointing readers to a free version of the next book in the series to get them on your mailing list. That second book is still available for purchase at an online ebook retailer, but to get it for free you have to sign up to his list.

At the time of this book, I'm in the process of testing this strategy.

Of course, on my website I offer the permafree book as an incentive to sign up for my list as well, and at the end of the Mailchimp funnel, I point the subscriber to the free Amazon book record page.

**TITLE PAGE**

This page has the title, subtitle, author, and publisher of the book. Pick up any paperback novel and you'll find a pretty standard version of this page.

The title page should be centered with the title on top and Author Name underneath.

**COPYRIGHT PAGE**

Usually the verso of the title page. That's an old-school publishing way of saying it's on the backside of the title page on the left as you look at the book.

This page contains the copyright notice, publication infor-mation, legalese, and the book's ISBN. Credits for design, editing, and illustration can be included on the copyright page.

## DEDICATION PAGE

Not every book carries a dedication. If you include one, it should come after the copyright page.

This is where you're allowed some leeway in making what you write all about you and who you're dedicating the book to. Make it quick and fun. One or two lines should do.

## TABLE OF CONTENTS PAGE

In non-fiction, this page lists all the sections and chapters. Its job is to help the reader navigate the book.

Regardless, most fiction novels I've read and published don't include a Table of Contents for the simple reason that they'd just be a list of Chapters—1, 2, 3. . .

## SECOND HALF TITLE

If you have a lot of front matter pages—acknowledgements, foreword, etc.—a half title page can be added before the beginning of the body of the book to remind the reader.

The page after it is usually blank and precedes the body of the book.

# BODY BASICS

## WISK

"If I said you had a beautiful body, would you. . .? That's just lame." — Steve Windsor

## BODY

I mentioned this earlier, but there are some more details to it.

This is the main portion or body of the book. For now, I've been splitting my stories into very logical four-part structures to signal each new phase of the novel. There are as many ways to structure the body section of a novel as there are stories, but there are some basic guidelines.

## PART OPENING PAGE

Both fiction and nonfiction books are often divided into parts or sections when there's a large enough separation of information to warrant it.

I mentioned parts earlier, but some reasons to create parts in your novel are if you jump from past to present day, or if you want to make a logical split between structural elements, worlds, or realms in your story.

## CHAPTER OPENING PAGE

Most fiction books are divided into chapters to provide the reader a way to chunk up the information and follow the story. Chapter opening pages are found in most novels, and they can be on the right or left hand pages. (Section titles are always on the recto—right.)

Many times, chapter and section titles are indented down the page a set number of lines. The chapter title is about a quarter of the way down the page and the text is halfway. This is personal preference and can be adjusted in Scrivener's Formatting setting in the Compile feature.

## LAST PAGE

The last page can be as simple as text that says "The End" after the last words. However, it's kind of a letdown to the reader when they just spent 5-10 hours of their lives getting to know your characters. So the last page is a great place to thank them for that effort.

It can be as simple as saying, "Congratulations! You just finished reading *JUMP*, the first book in *The Fallen* series, turn the page to get access to book 2." That does a couple of things—thanks your reader and offers them something else to read.

Remember, we're trying to make them a long term fan, so let's explore how to do that in the back matter.

# BACK MATTER BASICS

## WISK

"If you don't have a good front, a great backside matters even more." — Steve Windsor

## CREATING BACK MATTER

Back matter is everything that comes after the end of the story. It can be anything you might want your reader to know about the book or you.

Remember, your book is also a marketing piece designed to get you long-time readers—subscribers to your email list—so we're going to put content in there to convert your one-time reader into a long term fan.

There isn't a specific order that back matter should be in, but here are some suggestions.

## NEXT BOOK COVER

In a series, I start right out by offering a reader who's made it all the way through the book—they obviously liked it—a quick peek at the next book in the series' book cover, and then follow that up with a teaser page that has an excerpt or the beginning few pages of the next book.

Hard to do if you haven't written the next book, but you can also write out a summary of the unwritten book to put in here. In fact, this is one of the reasons I created my entire series of book covers and summaries early on.

## NEXT BOOK TEASER

The teaser is as many pages of the next book in the series as it takes to hook a reader into at least taking a look at it. If you don't have that, a summary you've written will do the same job.

## REVIEW REQUEST

The heart and soul of a successful book on Amazon will be measured in reviews. It's unfortunate that only the people who take time to review your book will be the determining factor of how successful it is, but reviews are huge.

So on this page you're going to do your best to create a compelling reason—plea, beg, borrow, steal, anything you can to convince an exhausted reader to do one more thing—to leave you a review. Preferably, a positive one.

People put puppy pics, smiley faces, anything they can.

I'm not that "fuzzy," so I usually have one of my characters in the book ask in a creative way. (Read that as rough and raw.)

## ABOUT THE AUTHOR

This page is exactly what it says. It should contain contact information like your email address, Twitter handle, Facebook page, and website address with an invitation to connect with the author—you.

And that's it, your book's "done." Not quite. . .

# COMPILING YOUR BOOK

## WISK

"I said compiling, not composting." — Steve Windsor

## WHAT'S COMPILING?

Okay, we've written, *edited*, and formatted our book into nice clean sections, chapters, scenes, and paragraphs, and arranged all of them into logical front, body, and back parts. Now let's talk about producing the files that KDP and CreateSpace need in order for you to publish your book with them.

### Compiling in Scrivener

One of the truly monstrous powers of Scrivener is the Compile feature. It's also the part that I mentioned scaring the hell out of most new application users.

**Compiling is simply the act of taking all of the wonderful words you've written and turning them into the encoded files that the various e-readers and applications can understand.** For KDP that's a .mobi file and for CreateSpace it's a printable .pdf.

# COMPILING IN SCRIVENER

Compiling is as easy and as difficult as organizing your book correctly in the binder, clicking the FILE > COMPILE menu item, and then filling out each and every box in the Compile pop-up box Settings.

I'm going to say Compile is manageable. Not easy, but not beyond the skills of a motivated author such as yourself.

## KDP BASIC COMPILE SETTINGS

### KDP

In order to produce a custom .mobi file to upload to our KDP book record, we'll have to do a couple preliminary things.

First, **install the KindleGen plugin for Scrivener**.

There's a long, lengthy and boring description of what it does on the Amazon download page. All you need to know is that in order to make Scrivener output a .mobi file for KDP, you'll need to install the KindleGen app.

Search the Internet for the KindleGen application or get it here:

<u>https://authorbasics.com/kgen</u>

Unzip or unarchive the file to a folder location of your choosing, making sure to remember where that folder is.

Open up the Compile function with the button at the top-center of Scrivener's application screen or by going to the FILE > COMPILE menu item and changing the Compile For setting to .mobi.

Then we need to skip down the list of Compile settings to "KindleGen."

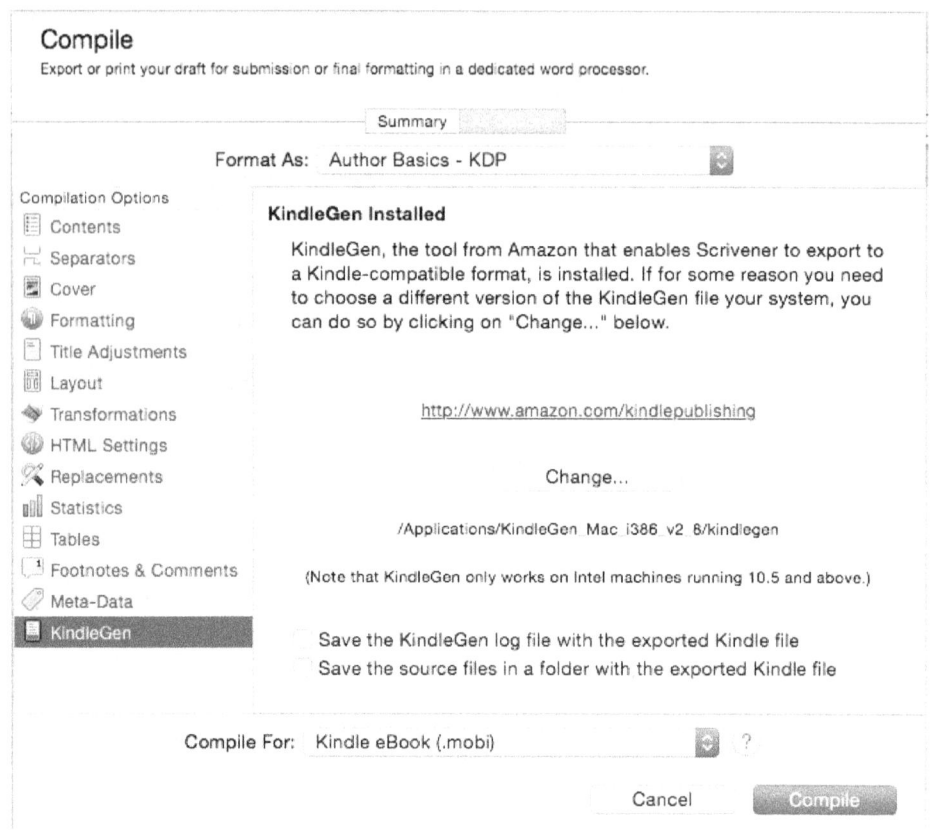

Inside the KindleGen setting, there's one button you're concerned with—"Change." Click it and point to the location of the KindleGen application you downloaded, and then click the "KindleGen" app. Click okay or open.

Now KindleGen is installed in Scrivener and we can get to work on creating a custom setting.

**Compile For**

It's a pop-down menu at the bottom of the Scrivener Compile screen. You can see it in the image above.

The reason we skipped down to the KindleGen setting, is that in order to select "Kindle eBook (.mobi)" from this drop-down menu, we needed to install KindleGen. So select that .mobi setting now.

Now we're ready to create a custom compile setting.

You can create a custom compile setting inside the For-mat-As: settings box.

In this pop-down menu you'll find a list of standard tem-plates you could use to compile your manuscript. I always choose to make a custom preset by **clicking Manage Compile Format Presets**, because that's just how I am. If you wanted to, you could choose one of the "Novel" settings, but I guarantee you're going to customize them anyway.

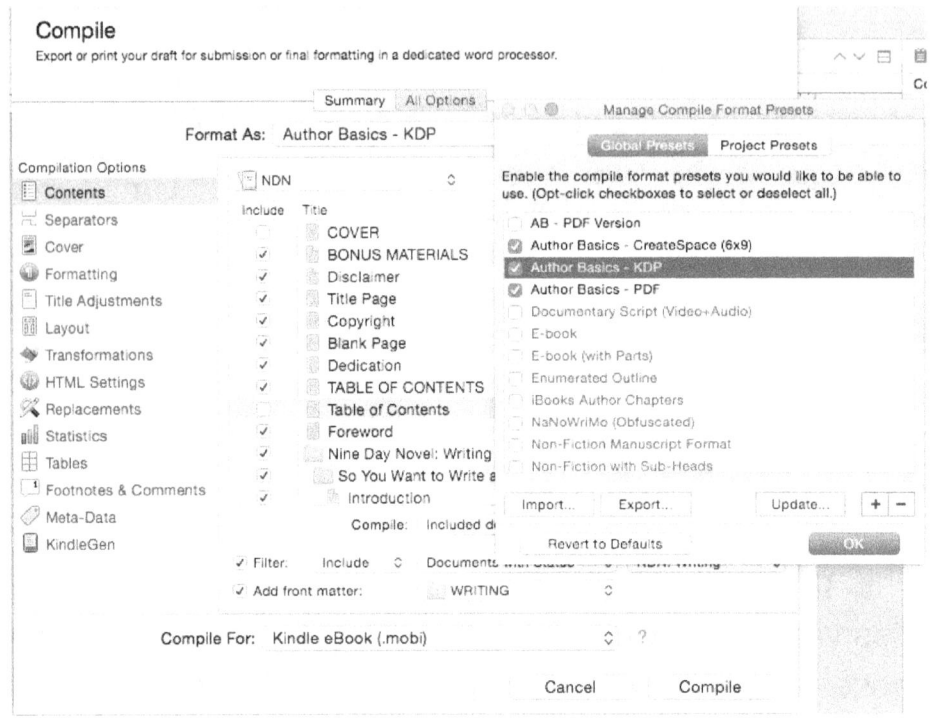

Make a new preset by clicking on the "+" sign in the lower righthand corner. I name mine by series/genre and destination or purpose. (Example: The Fallen Series — KDP.) Name yours something that makes sense and for which you can easily recall its purpose. Then click "okay" and we'll get started customizing your preset.

## Contents

This is where you select which folders and documents to include or exclude from your compiled file, whether to print each document "as-is" (the way you formatted it in your editor) or let the Compile > Formatting section's settings determine how your text will look.

**I do all my formatting inside Compile. I suggest you do as well.**

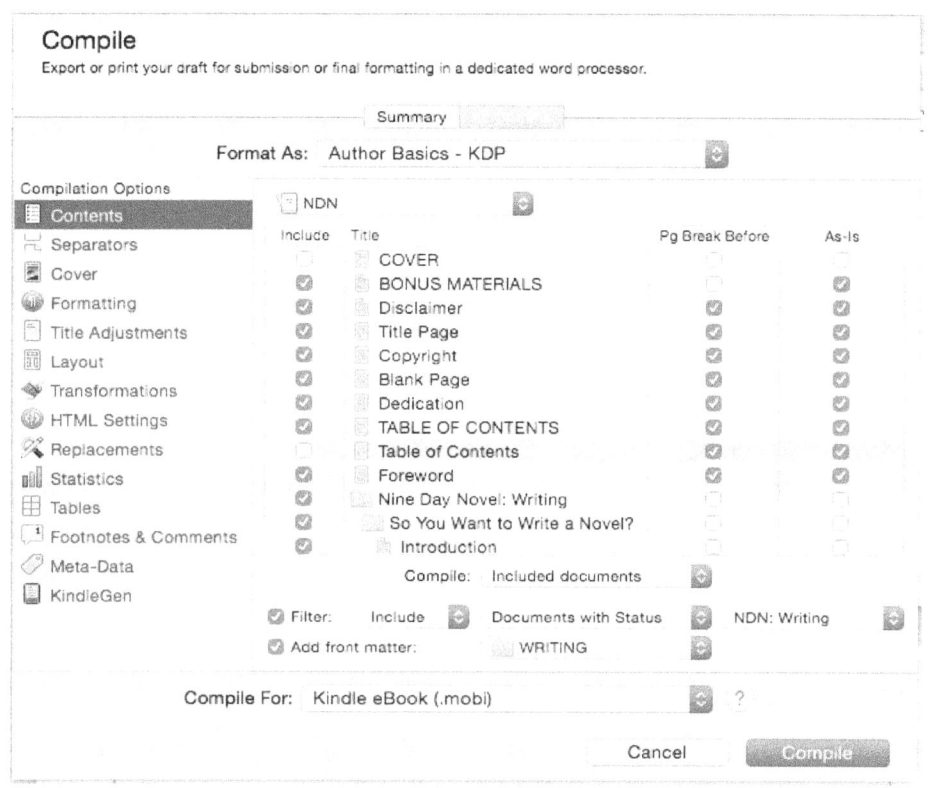

There are advanced include/exclude functions at the bottom, for selecting or excluding certain classes of documents. For now, we'll assume you have one book in your file and you want most of the folders and documents you created in your final file. So under the little "Compile" drop-down menu item at the bottom of the window, select "All."

Select which documents you want and how they'll look

with the check boxes in the window to their right. Hint: I put manual page breaks before all of my front matter docs, because they're documents and would only have a blank line space if I didn't.

Quick Tip: If you want to select all your files manually, you can select or deselect all the files at once by holding down the "option" key and clicking one of the checkboxes to the left of any file.

## Separators

**Text Separator**—This is where you determine what goes between adjacent documents. Remember our spacing between scenes? This is what controls that. Select "Blank Line."

**Folder Separator**—This is where a separator between your Section folder and your Chapter subfolders is defined. Select "Section Break" to make the very first chapter in a Section start on the next page after your Section title page.

**Folder and Text Separator**—This setting determines what goes between your folder (chapter) and the very first scene. To keep it simple, I select "Empty Line."

**Text and Folder Separator**—This setting determines the break between the last word of the last scene in a chapter and the next section or chapter following it. I choose "Section Break" to make the next section or chapter start on a fresh page.

At the end, your Separators sections should look like this:

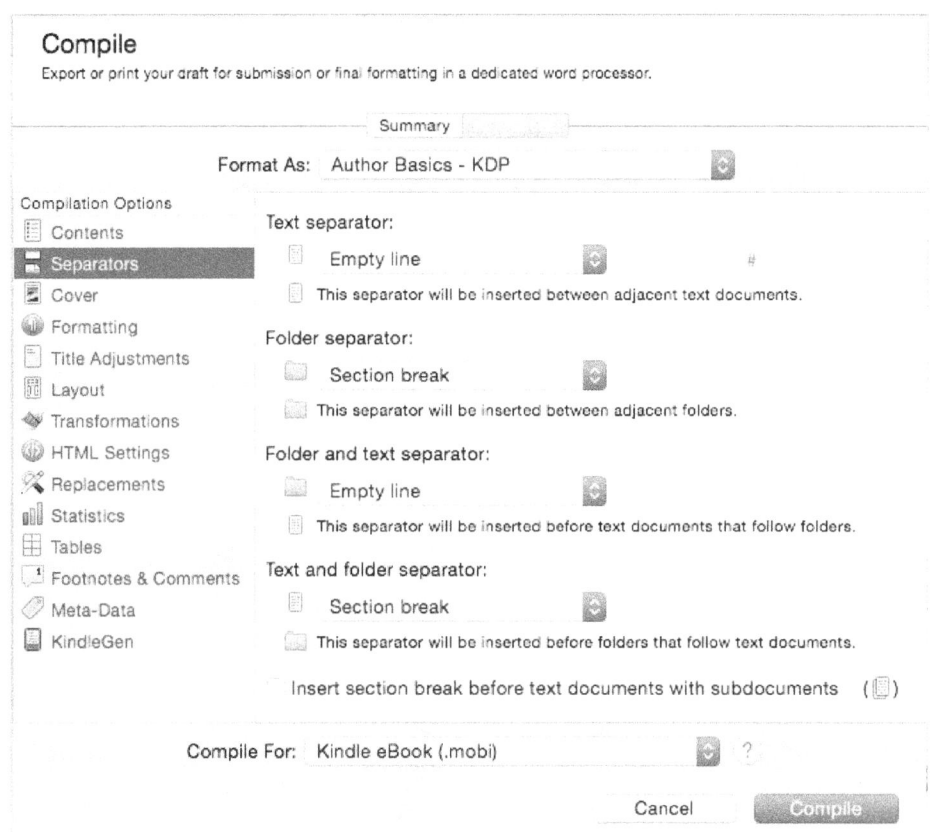

## Cover

NOTE: You don't need to put your cover inside a docu-ment in order for it to show up in your KDP .mobi file, because this setting selects an image to include in the compiled .mobi.

If you haven't yet, you'll need to import your saved cover .jpeg or .png to the binder. I make a folder for all my images in my binder, just below all of my book internals. Then I import images into that folder with the FILE > IMPORT > FILES. . . menu item.

The Cover setting in Compile recognizes images and when you select the Cover Image dropdown menu, all the images in your binder appear and you can select your cover.

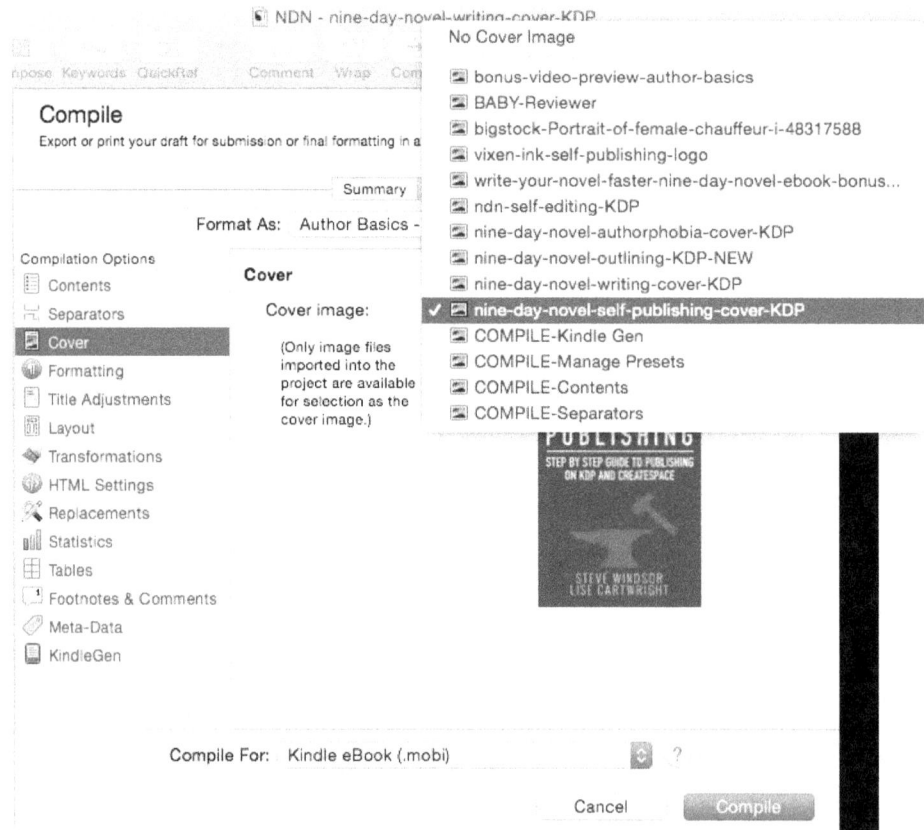

## Formatting

This section's settings get a little . . . wild. Wild as in MS Word powerful/complicated. It's where the titles and text of folders, subfolders, and text documents are all format-ted and controlled. It's extremely powerful and extremely complicated to explain.

There's two sections to it. The top, where you see the "Levels"—all the folders and documents that represent your sections, chapters, and documents. In that top pane you can select whether Scrivener will display the title and/ or the text for a type of item. "Title" and "Text" click boxes are the only ones we'll mess with; leave the others blank.

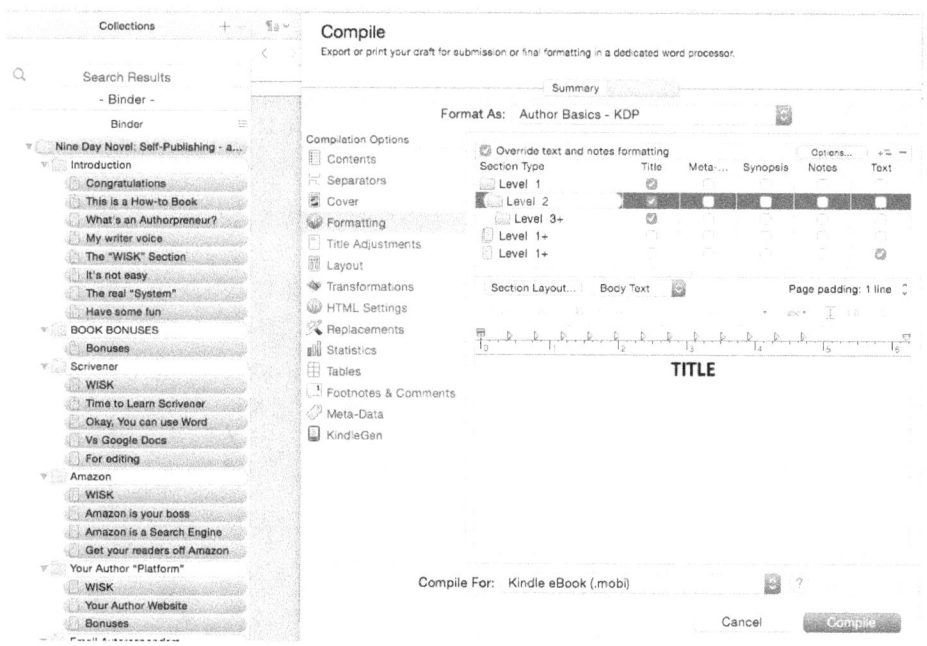

Just remember this—the top-level folder usually translates to a section, the next level folder is chapters, and the third is sub-chapters (which I don't use so I remove this one by highlighting it and clicking the "-" (minus) button in the upper right hand corner). By selecting the "Title" click box for folders, you tell Scrivener to render and print the titles that are on those folders in the binder —they turn into your chapter titles.

There's only one level of document file you should concern yourself with and that's the single document. That's the one that controls your text documents or, as we've been referring to them, your scenes. The body of your text is controlled by selecting the Text click box for this item, highlighting its row, and then clicking in the bottom pane of the Formatting window.

Then click the little "A" icon. That's the font formatting for the text that will be your paragraphs and body text. Easier than it sounds.

**Title Adjustments**

This setting adjusts title prefixes and suffixes that were selected in the Formatting section. I usually click the first two to not use prefixes and suffixes in the front matter. Regardless, we shouldn't have anything in our file that points to prefixes and suffixes.

## Layout

For my fiction books, I leave all these settings unchecked.

## Transformations

These are the items I check under this setting. . .

- **Convert ellipses to triple periods**—This does what it says. Most fiction novels use triple periods with single spaces between them for ellipses functionality, like this: ". . ."

- **Remove trailing white spaces from documents**—If you accidentally put an extra carriage return at the end of a document (happens all the time), this removes that white space.
- **Convert multiple spaces to single spaces**—Remember the old double space between sentences rule? This turns any accidental double space back into a single one. Very useful.

There are a host of other settings, but these do the bulk of what you need to get done.

## HTML Settings

Select the setting under Links—Convert Scrivener links to HTML links, though all of the links in your file should be HTML links.

## Replacements

Project Replacements are project wide and affect every compile preset you create. If you want to make a replacement that will only affect an individual compile preset—one that will only affect the current Format As setting—make a "Preset Replacement."

## Statistics

Since we aren't going to put any statistics in our novel, deselect all of these. They don't matter to us.

## Tables

You don't have tables in your fiction novel, do you? Deselect everything.

## Footnotes & Comments

Ditto with footnotes. We don't have them. They're boring.

## Meta-Data

The only information I put in here are Title, Author, Publisher, and Language.

## KindleGen

Remember this setting? You should've installed the KindleGen application and the path to it should show up above the button. Don't change anything if you've already done that. If not, scroll up or turn back to the "install the KindleGen plugin for Scrivener" section and get the application installed.

Exhausted? Good, you're almost done.

Don't click compile just yet! You went to all that trouble detailing how your book should look, and we'd hate to have to repeat it. So we're going to save all these settings to the Format As: custom preset we created at the beginning.

Drop down the box next to Format As and **select Manage Compile Format Presets**. Make sure the one you created is highlighted and click the "Update" button at the bottom of the window. Overwrite it and now you have a preset that you can simply select the next time you want to compile your novel or another one just like it to KDP.

Bam! On to CreateSpace compile settings.

Confused or lost? Yes, I know that Compile is difficult at first, so I've put together a tutorial video as a bonus to walk you through it in real time.

**Step 1** - https://authorbasics.com/join/ of our Awesome Author community at Author Basics

**Step 2** - Enjoy the video tutorials at:

https://authorbasics.com/ndn-sp-bv/

**CREATESPACE BASIC COMPILE SETTINGS**

**Format-As:**

Once again, we're going to make a custom preset for CreateSpace by clicking Manage Compile Format Presets.

Create a new preset by clicking on the "+" sign in the lower righthand corner. I now name my preset "The Fallen — CS" to represent my entire Fallen fiction series and denote that this preset is to compile them for Create-Space. Customize yours and click "okay," and then get started customizing your new print preset.

**Compile For**

Even though this file will need to be a .pdf for Create-Space, we're going to select "Print" as our option here.

**Contents**

If you recall, this is where you selected which folders and documents to include or exclude from your compiled file.

If you haven't done anything in Compile since you made the above KDP preset, the list of included files should be the same. If not, go back through and select the ones you want and how you want them displayed, including page break settings.

Once again, under the little "Compile" drop-down menu item at the bottom of the window, make sure "All" is the option.

## Print Settings

This setting didn't exist when we chose the Kindle eBook (.mobi) Compile For: setting. Right now, we just want the Layout Type to be set to Publishing, and both Links checkboxes to be blank.

## Separators

These settings are the same as KDP, but I'll list them out anyway so you don't have to jump back and forth in the document or book.

**Text Separator**—This is where you determine what goes between adjacent documents. Remember our spacing between scenes? This is what controls that. Select "Blank Line."

**Folder Separator**—This is where a separator between your Section Folder and your Chapter subfolders is defined. Select "Section Break" to make the very first chapter in a section start on the next page after your section title page.

**Folder and Text Separator**—This setting determines

what goes between your folder (chapter) and the very first scene. To keep it simple, I select "Empty Line."

**Text and Folder Separator**—This setting determines the break between the last scene in a chapter and the next section or chapter following it. I choose "Section Break" to make the next section or chapter start on a fresh page.

## Cover

This selection doesn't exist under the Format As "Print" setting. It won't be included in your CreateSpace internals file. You'll upload a separate .pdf of your front and back cover combined for your print book cover. More later. . .

## Formatting

These settings should be the same as your KDP settings. The only difference is that if you used any colors in your titles or text settings, they'll render as black and white when we upload to CreateSpace.

This is where the titles and text of folders, subfolders, and text documents are all formatted and controlled. There are two main sections to it. The top, where you see the "Levels"—all the folders and documents that represent your sections, chapters, and documents. In that top pane you can select whether Scrivener will display the title and/or the text for a type of item.

Just remember that the top-level folder is usually a section, the next level folder is chapters, and the third is sub-chapters (which I don't use and you probably won't either). By selecting the "Title" click box for these folders, you tell Scrivener to render and print the binder titles on the folders in the binder outline.

The single file document is for your paragraph and body text. The body of your text is controlled by selecting the Text click box for this item, and then clicking in the bottom pane of the Formatting window.

Then click the little "A" icon and that's the font formatting for the text that will be your paragraphs and body text.

**Title Adjustments**

This setting adjusts title prefixes and suffixes that were selected in the Formatting section. I usually click the first two, to not use prefixes and suffixes in front matter.

**Layout**

Under this section I check Use Hyphenation so words that span lines will get a hyphen. I also check Replace empty line separators that fall across pages with a "***".

This is so that any scene/document break that will result

in an empty line at the top or bottom of a physical page gets replaced with those characters. It looks better and doesn't leave the reader wondering why the first line of a page is spaced down farther than the adjacent page.

## Transformations

These are the items I check under this setting.

- Convert ellipses to triple periods—This does what it says. Most fiction novels use triple periods with single spaces between them for ellipses functionality.
- Remove trailing white spaces from documents—If you accidentally put an extra carriage return at the end of a document, this removes that white space.
- Convert multiple spaces to single spaces—Remember the old double space between sentences? This turns any accidental double space back into a single one.
- Convert Underlines to Italics—Links are usually underlined and if you have them in your file for KDP, this will remove them.
- Remove text color—CreateSpace will be a black and white file anyway.
- Remove all hyperlinks—You can't have hyperlinks in a print book.

There are a host of other settings, but these do what you need to get done.

## Replacements

Project Replacements are project wide and affect every compile preset you create. If you want to make a replacement that will only affect the current file's Format As setting, make a Preset Replacement.

## Statistics

Deselect all.

## Tables

Deselect everything.

## Footnotes & Comments

Select everything that says "Remove."

## Page Settings

This is where things get . . . interesting. This setting basically controls the physical dimensions of the outside of your book. It also controls the internal margins and the header and footer text, including page numbering location.

We're going to take a little break and talk about book

sizes, but before that, save all these settings again to the Format As: custom preset we created at the beginning.

Drop down the box next to Format As and select Manage Compile Format Presets. Make sure the one you created is highlighted and click the "Update" button at the bottom of the window. Overwrite it and now you have a preset that you can simply select the next time you want to compile your novel or another one just like it for CreateSpace.

## BOOK SIZES

I'll keep this short and simple. There are so many "standard" trim sizes for novels out there that I had to wonder how they could call them standard at all.

Mass market fiction novels—the ones you see in drugstore shelves—are usually 4.25" x 7" trim sizes. That being said, CreateSpace doesn't offer that trim size as an option. So the next best—most popular—trim sizes are 5" x 8" and 5.25" x 8". Some do 6"x9", but that's more popular as non-fiction.

I printed *The Fallen* series in 5.25" x 8" because I took out a tape measure and measured *The Hunger Games* paperbacks.

However, you get to choose. My advice is to pick one and stick with it for all your novels, because your Scrivener settings can be reused over and over again. You'll fine-tune and dial in the trim size, fonts, word counts, page numbering, and margins that work well for the size, and then you don't have to mess with them any more.

We'll do that as soon as we get back to our Compile Print setting for our CreateSpace preset.

There's another reason to stick with your trim size settings. Because once you've chosen a trim size for your book and received an ISBN number for that title, the trim size is part of the ISBN and can't be changed.

This is CreateSpace's message should you desire a new trim size: "The trim size and interior type are associated with your book's ISBN and cannot be changed."

That seems like a pretty good reason to get it right the first time.

## CREATESPACE COMPILE SETTINGS CONTINUED

Back to our Compile settings. FILE > COMPILE, and then select the "Page Settings" tab on the left.

Deselect Use project Page Setup Settings and click the Page Setup button.

This is where you'll define the trim size you've selected.

As an example, let's just pick an easy 5" x 8" trim size.

The setting inside that you're concerned with is Paper Size > Manage Custom Sizes. Click on the "+" sign in the lower left to add a custom page size. Then enter 5.25" in the width column and 8" in the height column and set all the margins to "0." (The reason for the zero margins is that we'll control those back in the main Print settings window.)

Click Okay and you're back at the main Print Settings window.

**Margins**

Margins are tricky, because they depend on your page count and CreateSpace has some minimum margins so that text doesn't get lost in the gutter. (That's the spine space between the right and left pages.) And as your page count goes up, more and more of the visible page is lost to the bend in the spine.

The margins that work for my novels at 5.25" x 8" and 325 to 375 pages are—top .5", bottom
.7", left .75" (which means the gutter in the center), and right . 35" (which actually means the outer edge of either page; whether it's the left or right page doesn't matter).

Now hang on, because we're almost there.

**Header and Footer Print Settings**

If you want to put page numbers in your novel—and who wouldn't because it's not only professional-looking, but coincidentally very useful to the reader—then you'll do that in the little boxes below the Header Footer section in the Compile Print Settings.

The "Header and Footer" tab at the bottom of that page

represents what will show up on the right hand pages, and the "Facing Pages" tab represents what will show up on the left hand pages. There's all kinds of information from your file that you can put in these boxes, but for our basic needs, "<$p>" (minus the quotations), is what you put so that Scrivener numbers each page with its correct value.

In Header and Footer (right hand), I have that code in the lower right hand box—the outside of the footer of the right hand page. And on the Facing Pages tab (the left hand pages), I have the code in the lower left hand footer box. That way my page numbers are on the outer edge of my pages as you look at the two pages of an open book.

**First Pages Tab**

The trouble we have now is that we have all that front matter that really isn't part of the page numbering for the actual novel. The "First Pages" tab tells Scrivener how we want to handle that.

Click the Different First Pages Header and Footer check-box and set the page count, "Start Regular Header and Footer on:" to Automatic. This will skip the front matter documents in the page count and start page number one on the first page of the text of your novel.

Leave all the value boxes in the First Pages tab blank, or

if you wanted to put Roman numerals on the front matter pages—a common practice—you could insert this code "< $p-r>" without the quotations. I put that in the middle footer box to insert a lowercase Roman numeral on the bottom center of my front matter pages.

**Header and Footer Fonts**

The font settings for your header and footer are at the bottom of the page and they control the size and font of that text code we just inserted to add page numbering. You can play with them, but I make them smaller than my body font by one or two points. So if my body is 11 point, they're around 9 point.

**Quick Font Override**

This does what the explanation says and wipes out all other fonts and changes them to a single font . . . every-where. Overriding everything is not what I want, so I never use this.

**Make sure you save your preset again before you click that final Compile button or you'll lose all this customization work**. Once that's done, click the Compile button.

When Scrivener is done rendering the file, it'll ask you where you want to "print" to. After all this is a Format As:

Print Compile setting that we chose, isn't it? Kinda. . .

On the next screen you're presented with, the button says "Print," but we don't actually want to *print* the entire book; we want to generate a .pdf file for print purposes. So in the lower left corner of the window is a dropdown menu and when you click it you can select "Save as PDF." Then Scrivener will ask you what you want to name that .pdf file and where you want to save it.

And that, as they say, is that. Now you have your .pdf for CreateSpace. It feels more painful to read the instructions for it than it is to go through an actual compile, but after you've done it a few times, it's pretty "easy."

# BOOK COVERS

## WISK

"Don't judge a book by its cover? Who told you that?" —
Steve Windsor

## BOOK COVER PURPOSE

We all observe and judge everything to get our first impression of whether or not we like something. Malcolm Gladwell wrote an entire book, *Blink*, about how we make snap decisions in an instant about most things in our lives. Book covers are no different.

Book cover creation is such a huge topic that I'm considering writing an entire book on it. That being said, your book cover has one purpose—get a prospective reader to take a closer look at your book.

You want to present a clear and compelling reason for someone to slow down their Amazon power-browsing session long enough to read your title, and then potentially read your book's description, look inside at some sample content, or just buy it right then and there.

Many authors are so used to seeing physical books that they forget the largest size most readers will ever see a book cover is as a tiny little image on an Amazon book listing page. And it's even smaller in the top 100 and Hot New Releases sections.

At minimum, and at those small sizes, you want your title to be legible and your cover to be contrasted enough that someone can roughly make out what the image on the front is. So make sure, as you look at your proposed cover, to look at it in a small size as well as that big beautiful one your designer sent you.

There's a balance between fun and functional when it comes to covers.

Make your main title as big as possible and clearly legible. Then go for a cool, genre-pertinent image that has contrasted colors. If you want to see what works for a cover, look at the top 5-10 books in the categories you researched for your book. They'll give you a good idea of what kind of book covers are on the best selling books you're competing with.

**WHERE TO GET BOOK COVERS**

Here are some places to get decent book covers, including my own take on having used each one.

Fiverr.com—It's hit or miss but inexpensive if you're on a tight budget. $5-$50

99design contests—For $299, designers bid on your project. You can get a pretty good cover and you can get a mediocre one, depending on how well you run your contest.

Elance.com—Hire a freelance designer to design a cover to your specifications. $250-$500

Do it yourself

DIY Book Covers, by the awesome indie book cover designer, Derek Murphy, has some great Word template covers. If you have moderate technical skills, you can customize them to suit your needs. Currently $87.

KD Cover Kit—I use their pre-made layered Photoshop files as a starting point to design all my own covers and make custom covers for clients. You need to know Photoshop . . . well.

steve@authorbasics.com—If you don't like any of those options and/or you aren't familiar with Photoshop, you can hire me to make an awesome print and eBook cover for you.

# THE SERIES BOOK COVER

A quick note. For a series of books, it's important that they be branded/designed similarly so that potential readers can spot them as being related to a book they may have already read.

*The Fallen* series covers, written by yours truly, are a good example of design consistency across a series of covers. An even better one is the *JET* series, written by <u>Russell Blake</u>. He's basically taken over the Pulp Thriller category with his books, and when you look at them, there's no mistaking that all of his books are in the same series.

## BOOK COVER IMAGE REQUIREMENTS

Regardless of how or where you get your book cover designed, here are the details of what files you will need to have.

## KDP

At minimum you need a (72dpi) .jpg file that is preferably 2820x4500 pixels (at the moment, Amazon's largest allowable) in size. This is so that Amazon can scale it to all the sizes it will use in various places around its site and on the Internet. A larger original file helps your image maintain quality as it's being scaled.

## CreateSpace

CreateSpace requires that you submit a 300dpi .pdf file to specific specifications to use as your printable front, spine, and back book cover. Forget all the talk about CMYK as RGB coloring works perfectly fine for your printed book covers.

Information you'll need to provide a designer so they can create a cover for you that meets CreateSpace's specifications are:

- Your book's trim size that we mentioned earlier—5"x8," for example.
- Number of physical pages in the Create-Space PDF we made earlier. This is so your designer can download the CreateSpace book cover design template at www.create-space.com/Help/Book/Artwork.do to use as a guide.

The template helps a designer size the design file, and then place text, images, and graphics in the "safe" printable areas on your cover. And all that is to ensure that the spine, trimmed edges, and/or the bar code don't obscure vital information.

Other information you may need to give a designer.

The information on the front of your cover must contain at minimum the title, subtitle, and author name. The back cover should, but doesn't have to, have a summary of your novel, the title, subtitle, author photo, author bio, publisher logo, and a way to contact the author, such as the website address.

Believe it or not, all of this information is marketing material. It helps potential readers figure out if your book's worthy of 10 hours of their lives spent reading it.

Speaking of marketing. . .

# PRE-MARKETING

## WISK

"People! Why you no buy my book?" — I'll let author James H. Mayfield (Holger Maiväli's) website quote hijack this one.

## SWITCHING TO MARKETING

Okay, we're going to switch gears a little bit, because of all that compiling and book building. . . I know it seems brutal, but in practice, compiling and book production are easier than the explanations.

Once you have your internal files for KDP (.mobi) and CreateSpace (.pdf) and you have book cover files for them both as well (.jpg or .png for KDP and .pdf cover file for CreateSpace), we need to think a little bit about marketing. In reality, we should've been thinking about marketing from the very beginning, even before we wrote our book, but that's not how most of us start this journey.

Fiction is different from non-fiction book marketing. And in order to write compelling fiction stories, you have to first give a rip about the kind of story you're trying to write.

Solving boredom is different from answering questions about subjects and providing how-to information in non-fiction books.

Emotion, intensity, and passion are hard to fake, and fiction storytelling needs that feel to be entertaining and authentic.

So, yes, picking profitable genres, finding niche categories, and titling and creating a keyword rich description for your book are important, but I believe they need to be within the bounds of stories that you find irresistible to tell in the first place.

Since marketing is more art than science, we'll deal with the minimum steps you can take to make sure that your book lands in front of as many potential reader searches as possible.

And those steps are finding categories and niches you can target, searching for keywords that are popular in those categories, titling your book, and writing a description that sells.

If you remember, marketing is nothing more than everything you do to attract qualified traffic to view your book and have the opportunity to buy it. Category and keyword targeting are two of the first things we can optimize to help drive the correct traffic to your book's buy page.

## KINDLE SPY

First, I'm going to introduce you to another invaluable tool to help you market your books.

## <u>Kindle Spy</u>

Kindle Spy lets you browse any category in the Amazon Kindle marketplace, and in the background it gathers relevant information about the best sellers in that category. It shows you the breakdown of that category and the potential profit you could make there, along with a breakdown of each individual book's performance.

The application is a Chrome browser extension that's compatible with both PC & Mac. It also works with Firefox. At the time of this publication, it only costs $47. Regardless, next to Scrivener, Kindle Spy is one of the best bangs for your author buck.

**Here's what it does.**

**Kindle Spy shows you all the details of each book in the top 100 of any Amazon Kindle category**. Title, number of pages, sales price, estimated monthly units sold, estimated monthly revenue, number of reviews, and the ranking of each individual book. It also gives you the averages of that information as well.

The Word Cloud feature allows you to see the most popular words in all the titles in that category. This is helpful in titling your books closely with the top books in a category.

New features have just been added to Kindle Spy, like the Popularity, Potential, and Competition section. Here, red, yellow, and green lights help you gauge your potential competition and the rewards your book can expect if you place it in that category.

Throw in the fact that you can also track any individual book's rankings over time to watch your competitor's books and your own, and Kindle Spy is insanely useful. It's one of my must have tools.

You can get your copy by visiting https://authorbasics.com/9zkr/.

## CATEGORIES SELECTION

Now, here are the details on how to use Kindle Spy effectively.

Category research used to be the biggest pain in the butt I had before I could select profitable and easy to rank categories for my books. Now, I browse Kindle eBooks categories on Amazon to find top-level categories that are close to my genre, and then I drill down into subcategories that seem most appropriate for my book.

When I find a category that seems likely, let's say Literature & Fiction > Dark Fantasy, I click into that category and then click on the Kindle Spy icon on the right of my browser tools bar and check out the competition, pricing, and keywords.

But how do you really determine what category is a good one to target? Actually, you'll find out, when we go over creating your book record on CreateSpace and KDP, that you need to identify *two* categories.

Here's what to look for in a category.

**Look for categories that have at least 10 books in the top 20 with rankings between 10,000 - 50,000.** If there are more than that with a ranking of 10,000 or less, the category is too competitive and you should find another. (These are rough guidelines that work, but even I break them if I can't find a "perfect" category.)

**A quick word on pricing.**

As far as pricing goes, you can see what the average for the category is in Kindle Spy, but also check out the top 5 titles and see how they've priced their books. Price yours similar to theirs, because the work of reader price sensitivity is right there in front of you.

Yes, there will be outliers in each category—higher and lower priced books—but the bulk of the books you as a new author must compete with are priced very close to each other.

Also check out how much total money a title is making, because books that are lower down the list may make more money with higher prices and fewer unit sales. Until you really are Stephen King, you won't be able to get away with charging $11.99 for a Kindle eBook.

Like I said, a lot of this is art, not science.

And that's it—quick and dirty. Sure, you can play around all day with tools, trying to get it perfect, but perfect isn't published and you can change categories later when you get a feel for where your books do well.

## KEYWORD SELECTION

Kindle Spy is pretty good at showing you which words authors are using in their titles, and that'll help you determine how to title your books to fit into a category. But you also get five keywords to add to your CreateSpace book record and seven on KDP.

**These keywords help place your book in front of reader searches.**

The new Kindle Spy features can help you with keyword searches as well.

Click the search icon in the lower left and type in one of the words that you think would be a good fit for your genre. For my example of a Dark Epic book, I typed in "Dark Epic." Up popped a long-tail keyword, "Dark Epic Fantasy." Disregarding that the quick look outlook from Kindle Spy was a big red button, signifying that the competition was too heavy, I clicked the "Analyze" button anyway.

Then Kindle Spy looked up all the books with Dark Epic Fantasy as a keyword and presented all the details mentioned before as if we were researching a category. As it turns out, it's a cutthroat category and I needed to look into changing one of the keywords for my titles.

By the way, you can also click column headings to sort the Kindle Spy records by sales, rank, and any other column you choose. It's fantastic if you want to see what the top ranked are charging for their books or any other tidbit of information that will help you choose keywords.

**A quick "cheat"**

Look at the descriptions of the top three books in your category. You can find keywords to use in those descriptions, too. If you're stuck, try looking at the most helpful reviews to find more keyword possibilities.

But there's another great application that will tell you exactly what long-tail keywords readers are searching for on Amazon—variations, volume of search traffic, everything.

## MERCHANT WORDS

Merchant Words is an application/service that searches unique keyword data across Amazon. They've catalogued over 20 million search phrases that Amazon visitors use everyday as they shop—which searches are the most popular and least popular.

**Keyword searching used to take me hours. It's now more like 10-15 minutes of concentrated research.**

One thing to remember with Merchant Words is that you should **only search in the "Kindle Store" or "Books" category for keywords**. Otherwise you'll find keywords that tell you what all shoppers on Amazon are looking for, not just readers.

You can see how Merchant Words works for free, but to get any useful functionality you'll have to purchase it.

The service normally costs $30/mo, but at the time of

publishing this book, there's a promotional deal to get it for $9/mo. It's a great value for the time it saves you. If it's still running, you can get that deal by clicking or visiting this URL:

https://www.merchantwords.com/offer/friendsofskip

Interestingly, searching on "Dark Epic" in Merchant Words yielded no search results, while searching on Dark Fantasy returned some great variations with the right search volumes.

**What are the "right" search volumes?**

Once again, this is a rule of experienced thumb, but try to find long-tail keywords that have between 1000 and 3000 searches. Remember, it's a guideline and as you get better, your gut instinct will become as good as the tools are. But at a minimum, choose keywords with no less than 1000 searches.

A good overall strategy is to use Kindle Spy's search tool to find some of the more commonly used words in a category, and then match that with your overarching keyword that pertains to your books.

For example, if your books were about mysteries, you might have a keyword of mystery novels. And if the most commonly used word (in titles) was King, then you'd want to search King + mystery novels.

## TITLING

Fiction book titles are all over the map and analyzing them after they're successful is completely subjective. That being said, there are indie authors raking in the dough by writing good books that are adorned with very genre-specific titles.

**Take a look at <u>Celia Kyle's books on Amazon</u>.**

They're a great example of putting keywords in the subtitles to map directly to the key phrases her genre's readers are searching on Amazon. The subtitle key phrase "BBW Paranormal Shapeshifter Romance" puts her books directly in front of several search terms. (By the way, BBW is Big Beautiful Woman.)

## BOOK DESCRIPTION

Your book description's job is to help a potential reader make a decision to buy your book. That's it. So let's just dive in and design a compelling book description.

### Headline

A one sentence headline tells the reader why they should read your book. In movies, it's called a log line—a one or two sentence summary of what your story's about.

A flawed protagonist undertakes a high-stakes quest against a strong antagonistic force. Will he or she survive it?

When Jack Remington is forced to fly to Africa to find his girlfriend's sister and rescue her from a tribe of cannibal pygmies, he'll either learn to quit his womanizing ways or risk losing the only one who can truly save him.

Close. . . Maybe it needs a little refining, but you get the point. **Hero, quest, antagonist, consequences, and leave a little mystery at the end.**

### Inciting incident

If you don't remember from the rest of the *Nine Day Novel* series, the inciting incident is the moment that everything in your hero's world changes forever.

Let's say the eternal playboy, in our story, Jack, is finally cornered by his long time girlfriend, who, despite convention, asks him to marry her. Only two ways to go from there.

A "no" means the jig is up and he's kicked out; a "yes" means he's trapped forever. What to do? Just then, his girlfriend's phone rings and her sister's friends in Africa inform her that the girl's gone missing.

"Oh, Jack, will you save her?"
"Anything to get out of marry—I mean, surely, darling."

And Jack's off to Africa, delaying the inevitable.

Example: Before Jack has to answer a surprise marriage proposal from his on-again-off-again girlfriend, she's informed that her only sister has gone missing in Africa. An ex-Congo fighter, Jack agrees to go retrieve her for his beloved. And he's on the next plane out of New York, headed for what he thinks is less trouble than dealing with a marriage proposal.

**Sprinkle in a little mystery. . .**

Unbeknownst to Jack, there's a mysterious woman on the flight with him. Beautiful and strangely familiar, she's not who she appears to be.

**Raise the stakes a little. . .**

When the plane encounters turbulence, several passengers begin vomiting blood, but as flight attendants rush out the medical supplies, our mysterious woman seems a bit too calm.

**Present your book as a universal theme. . .**

Jack's quest for adventure is about to come face to face with the only thing more powerful than fear—love. And though he doesn't know it, if he fails this time, there won't be another.

**Compare it to a successful book/movie. . .**

If you liked Humphrey Bogart and Lauren Bacall in *Casablanca*, and Michael Douglas and "what's her name" in *Romancing the Stone*, you'll love Jack Remington and Jenna Jensen in *Lovestruck in Liberia*.

**Throw in some social proof testimonials. . .**

Here's what readers are saying about *LiL*.

"I didn't know whether to love him or hate him, but by the end I didn't care. The adventure was worth it either way."

"I almost tore a page off when the she took off her. . . I don't want to spoil it!"

**Give them some stats to chew on. . .**

An Amazon bestseller for longer than it takes you to brush your teeth, you won't be able to get this 225 page love letter to film noir out of your dreams for weeks.

**And of course, a call to action (CTA). . .**

Hurry, before all trace of Jack and Jenna's love crashes and burns over the Atlantic, scroll up and click Buy Now.

Now, let's get that book uploaded to Kindle. . .

# KINDLE DIRECT PUBLISHING

## GET A KDP ACCOUNT.

Okay, that book description got your creative juices flowing again, but now we've got work to do.

**First, create a KDP account at <ins>https://kdp.amazon.com</ins>.**

Log in and take a look around the dashboard. The Bookshelf is where your published books will be and Reports is where you can obsess over your daily sales stats.

This is how and where you'll upload, maintain, and keep track of your eBooks published through Kindle Direct Publishing.

## AMAZON KINDLE PREVIEWER

Now that we have your internal files compiled and created, and your book cover files ready to go, you'll need to search for and download the <ins>Amazon Kindle Previewer Application</ins> and the <ins>Amazon Kindle Reading Application</ins>.

I use both of these applications to preview my .mobi file in order to make sure the compile process didn't munge up my files in some way. Trust me, it happens.

For your CreateSpace .pdf file, opening it in a PDF viewer is fine. We're going to use another verification method after we upload to CreateSpace and KDP, and we'll talk about that shortly.

# SETUP AND UPLOADING

## CREATE A NEW BOOK RECORD

Once logged into KDP, go to your Bookshelf tab and click the "Create new title" button. This will bring up all the settings that need to be filled in for your book.

## KDP SELECT OR NOT

There are two options you need to consider before uploading your eBook to KDP—whether you choose to participate in KDP Select or not.

### What is KDP Select?

KDP Select gives you five days to promote your book for free for every 90 days that you're enrolled in the program. It was Amazon's answer to so many other services letting authors host their books for free.

Their solution was to lock your book in, exclusively for sale with them, for 90 days. During those 90 days, you can't offer it anywhere else. After you use your five free days, your book will be back on the Amazon market for the price you set. During this 90-day period, your book will be available to Kindle Unlimited subscribers.

**What's Kindle Unlimited?**

Amazon subscribers can borrow eBooks on their Kindle devices for free for a month. When someone borrows your book, it used to be that you earned a set amount of money, like $1.40 a borrow. Amazon has since changed the rules to include the actual page count that a reader scrolls forward in your book.

Translation, you earn roughly $.006 (at the time of this publication) for every page a reader reads. When they implemented this option, my Kindle Unlimited royalties went down significantly and it lit a fire under me to get my books on other retail platforms.

**You don't have to enroll in KDP select, but it's the easiest way to offer your book for free on Kindle.**

Bottom line, Amazon wants exclusivity and they incentivize you to give it to them.

For 90 days, your book can't be offered for sale anywhere else (except on CreateSpace—Amazon). You can opt out before your 90 days is up if you want to, but once you're in it you have to wait for the full 90 days to offer your book elsewhere. If you enroll and don't turn off auto-renewal, your book will be enrolled for another 90 days.

Kindle Select is nice if you want to use a free launch strategy, and then inch your price up to your book's final price over the course of a couple of weeks.

We talk about this strategy in our 15 Day Book Launch Blueprint free eBook. You can get it at https://authorbasic-s.com/ukhs/

## TITLE

Enter the title or name of your eBook here.

## SUBTITLE

If your book has a subtitle, enter it here. **Your title and subtitle together must be fewer than 200 characters.** The subtitle will appear on your book's detail page, and must adhere to the same guidelines as your title.

## SERIES TITLE

You can choose if your eBook is part of a series. If so, you can enter a series title in this box. When you enter a series title, enter only the name of the series.

**To ensure customers can find all the books in the series, do not add the individual book title or volume number in the series title field, and make sure you use the same series title for all the books in your**

**series.**

Amazon states that books in a series with the same series title will automatically link and create a series landing page on Amazon.com, in order of volume numbers. I've found that I have to call KDP support to make sure it gets done.

The series setting improves the discoverability of all the books in your series by showing customers all of the books that make up the series on a single page.

## VOLUME

Books without a volume number will not appear on the series page, so make sure to number your books in the order that you want to see them listed and read. At the time of this publication, series pages are only available on Amazon.com.

## EDITION NUMBER

A version is a particular edition of a book. Identifying the version number helps readers know whether the book is the original edition, or if it contains updated content.

If this is the first time you have published this book, enter the number one (1). If the book was previously published and the version you are publishing contains significant changes, enter the number two (2) (and so on).

## PUBLISHER

Enter the publisher name that you would like listed for your eBook on the book's detail page. This can be an individual or company name.

It can also be left blank.

## DESCRIPTION

Like the copy on the inside flap of a hardcover book, the description tells readers a bit about your eBook. You can enter a description for your eBook that is between 30 and 4000 characters in length.

At this time, multimedia items such as embedded YouTube videos are not supported in the description.

**Note: The book description on your title's detail page may be delayed but should appear within 72 hours.**

You can use HTML in your book description. Here's an HTML example of a book description.

<h2><b>Love thriller books? "(<em>JUMP</em>) grabs you, shakes you, and spits you out . . . leaving you wanting more."</b></h2><h3><font><b>The State took almost

everything Jake Blake ever cared about. Tonight, they want everything else.</b></font></h3><p><b><em>** From Thriller Author Steve Windsor **</em></b></p><p>Seattle. One man is trapped on the roof of a tall scraper downtown. Six angry agents are threatening to "remand him to Protection." Jake knows that means he'll be tortured and killed. Every citizen knows that.</p><p>Hiding and on the run for the past two years, for Jake, it's the end of the lying. Now, there's only one easy way down off this scraper, and getting captured and killed . . . isn't it.</p><p>Welcome to a world where freedom means a person still has the power of choice. But most of those choices are between bad and worse.</p><p>The citizens of the future have assured their security . . . by giving up just about every freedom they ever had. And they also gave up the only means they ever had to resist.</p><p>There are no more guns in Jake Blake's version of eternity, buried or otherwise. And if there are? If a citizen decides to dig one up? Well, they might find themselves trapped between the "heaven" of a quick and easy death and the "hell" of a long and torturous judgement.</p><p>Because, as Jake likes to say to anyone who will listen to one of his rants, "Sooner or later the boot finds its way to everyone's neck."</p><p>But tonight is citizen Jake Blake's sooner, and this time . . . the neck under that boot is his.</p><p>Revenge for the daughter they took. Right now, it's about as tall an order as the top of this scraper. But depending on the last decision he'll ever make as a man. . . Jake doesn't know it yet, but the fate of this eternity—the one where he's standing on the ledge of a forty-eight story building—hangs in the balance.</p><p>In and out of reality and nightmare, in the end, Jake must find his own absolution. His own faith.</p><p>But no matter what happens next, if he doesn't figure himself out, humanity has one day left.</p><h2><font>The first religious thriller in <em>THE FALLEN</em> series</font></h2><p><em>JUMP</em> is a <b>fast-paced, action-packed psychological thriller</b> that explores the accepted beliefs of religion and reality against a backdrop of tyranny and dystopian existence.</p><p><font><b><em>"A 21st Century version of 1984 . . . only worse."</em></b></font></p><p><font><b><em>"You will root for the bad-guy."</em></b></font></p><p><em>THE FALLEN</em> series of books in order:</p><ul><li><em><b>JUMP</b>, THE FALLEN: Testament 1</em>, a Thriller Novel</li><li><em><b>FURY</b>, THE FALLEN: Testament 2</em>, a Thriller Novel </li><li><em><b>FAITH</b>, THE FALLEN: Testament 3</em>, a Thriller Novel </li><li><em><b>DOGG</b>, THE FALLEN: Testament 4</em>, a Thriller Novel</li><li><em><b>HOLE</b>, THE FALLEN: Testament 5</em>, a Thriller Novel</li><li><em><b>BURN</b>, THE FALLEN: Testament 6</em>, a Thriller Novel</li><li><em><b>LIVED</b>, THE FALLEN: Testament 7</em>, a Thriller Novel</li><li><em><b>LIFE</b>, THE FALLEN: Testament 8</em>, a Thriller Novel</li><li><em><b>RAIN</b>, THE FALLEN: Testament 9</em>, a Thriller Novel</

li><li><em><b>SALVATION</b>, THE FALLEN: Testament 10</em>, a Thriller Novel</li></ul><h2><b>If you love an <b>action-packed, wild and wicked thriller</b>, get your copy of <em>JUMP</em> now.</b></h2>

**UPDATE: Now, the <p></p> tag gives double spacing; if you remove it but do a single return in your KDP book description area, that works fine.**

If all that HTML talk made your eyes glaze over and roll back, here's an online, real-time HTML tool to help you create one.

Copy the above HTML and go paste it into this tool to see what it looks like.

http://www.onlinehtmleditor.net/

## CONTRIBUTORS

Author, editor, foreword, illustrator, introduction, narrator, photographer, preface, translator.

 At least one author name is required.

## LANGUAGE

Amazon has a list of languages. I choose English and it's worth discussing others, but the bulk of current Amazon royalties are for English titles. That being said, there are starving markets in Germany and Brazil that I know indie authors are translating their books into native languages for.

We'll get into new markets in another book, but currently my English language titles sell in US, UK, Australia, NZ, Japan, Germany, Spain, India, Canada, and Brazil.

## ISBN

You don't need an ISBN number to publish an eBook. Amazon gives your book an ASIN number to track it. Regardless, **don't use the ISBN from your print book in this box.**

If for some reason you absolutely want an ISBN for your eBook, you have to buy a separate, new ISBN, not the one you used for your print book.

## VERIFY PUBLISHING RIGHTS

Your work of fiction is an original work, isn't it? So you select "not a public domain work."

## CATEGORIES

Here's where it gets interesting again.

Remember those two categories that we researched before? This is where you'll select them. But there's a catch. You knew that was coming, right?

**For whatever reason, the KDP Categories don't match the Kindle ones that you can search on Amazon.** More "Fun with Dick and Jane" work and we have to try and come close to the ones that we found in our research.

There are a million Internet threads dealing with this, but most boil down to: It sucks and you have to guesstimate which one is closest to the category you want. If you're lucky enough to have the one you want listed exactly as it is on the Kindle store, count your blessings.

Find your two categories and select them.

## AGE RANGE

I don't mess with this one, but if you're publishing erotica you might want to specify an age range.

## KEYWORDS

Probably the second most important selection on the list.

In KDP you can enter up to seven keyword phrases and there doesn't seem to be a character limit on each one. (CreateSpace has a 25 character limit on each keyword.)

## RELEASE TIME

You don't want to go down the pre-order rabbit hole until you have a fan base to market a yet-to-be-written book to, so select "I am ready to publish my book."

## UPLOAD YOUR COVER

And here comes that beautiful cover you had created. "Browse for Image," find it, and upload it.

We are *not* using KDP's built-in cover creator.

## DIGITAL RIGHTS MANAGEMENT

We're not so much worried about people trying to steal our book as we are total and complete obscurity. Cross the "you're so popular people are stealing your book" bridge when you come to it.

Deselect—uncheck.

## UPLOAD YOUR BOOK FILE

This is where that hard work of compiling your .mobi file comes in. "Browse" for the file and upload it.

## PREVIEW YOUR BOOK

Surprisingly, **I *love* the online KDP eBook previewer**. It's a final sanity check after you upload your compiled .mobi file. Believe me, things can "happen," so use it to double check your file.

Then "Save and Continue" and you're taken to the "Rights and Pricing" tab.

## VERIFY YOUR PUBLISHING RIGHTS

Unless you don't have worldwide rights to publish your book under some sort of legal agreement, click "World-wide Rights."

## KDP PRICING SUPPORT

This is a beta service that attempts to help you figure out the correct price to use for your books based on similar ones. They show you a sweet spot which is supposed to be where authors make the most money.

I've found the tool to be useful, but each time I try to price as it suggests, sales plummet. I think it's an optimistically skewed tool. That's just me.

## KDP PRICING AND ROYALTY SPLITS

We have been over KDP Royalty Splits and this next section is where you select them on a country by country basis.

The cliff notes are that for a new title in a new genre, I'll launch a book at Free with KDP Select for two days and market the hell out of it to as many FREE book marketing sites as I can (we give away a list of those sites at https://authorbasics.com/0ytv/)and then switch it to .99 for 3-5 days, then $1.99 for 3-5 days, and so on until I get to the final price at which I want to keep the book.

The entire time I'm promoting it on Twitter, Facebook, my email marketing list, and to anyone I can find who'll listen.

**A word on country pricing. . .**

Currently, the bulk of my royalties come from the US, but 10-20% come from UK, Germany (.de), Canada (.ca), and Australia (.au), Brazil, India, and Spain, as I mentioned before. I try to price them all as multiples of a ".99" ending, and I have been known to cut Australia and Canada a slight break in pricing because they get jacked with a higher base pricing on their respective Amazon stores.

When you're making $100 total royalties—and I've been there—it doesn't seem like much, but scaling up, every $50-100 counts.

Regardless, KDP says it takes 12 hours for pricing updates to show up on your book's Kindle record. I've seen
it take much less time than that, so it's not an exact science.

## KINDLE MATCHBOOK

I have never seen this do much, but you can enroll your
print books in this and if a reader buys a print book, they
can get the Kindle book for the price you specify here.

## KINDLE BOOK LENDING

Enrolling in this lets readers—purchasers of your Kindle
eBook—lend it to "friends and family," whatever Amazon
deems that to mean. I do it, but I'm revamping my distribution strategies to rely less on all of Amazon's bells and
whistles and take my book's back into my own hands.

Can you feel that? We're almost done. . .

**Wait! Before you click the "Save and Publish" check-
box, read the next section.**

## KDP LAG TIMES

Before you click the the "Save and Publish" button, you
need to know this.

**After hitting Save & Publish, it will take about 12-24 hours, depending on what data you changed, for your book to be available on the Kindle store.** (12 to be available for sale, 24 for title, cover, and other core changes)

**During that time, you can't make changes to your book record—you can't even look at the details pages.** So make sure you've done everything—clicked every button, set every price correctly, everything. Because you're gonna lose a day of access to fix any problems.

This becomes a big issue when your book's description is messed up, or if you chose the wrong price or you mess up the timing on a tightly scheduled launch plan.

Finally, once you've filled all of that information in, click "Save and Publish" to submit your book to the Kindle Store.

.

# CREATESPACE

## GET A CREATESPACE ACCOUNT.

CreateSpace is Amazon's print on demand (physical books) subsidiary. It's one of the easiest and cheapest ways to sell your books as physical copies, not only to individuals, but to libraries and universities also.

If you want further incentive, CreateSpace represents almost 20% of our individual monthly book sales.

Visit www.createspace.com to get started.

## LINKING KINDLE AND PRINT EDITIONS

Many Kindle Direct Publishing (KDP) authors and publishers also have a physical edition published through CreateSpace or another publishing house.

Linking these various formats to one another in the Amazon catalog provides a better browsing experience for customers, so you'll want to make sure your Kindle and print edition titles and subtitles (if applicable) match exactly.

During the publishing process, KDP will attempt to match title, author name, and other title information to physical counterparts available in the Amazon catalog. This may take up to 24 hours after the title is live in the Kindle Store.

If you see your book linked to an incorrect edition, or if more than 48 hours have passed since your Kindle book went live and the print edition is still not linked, let KDP know by clicking the "Contact Us" button when logged into your KDP account (you'll see it once you click on "Help" from the top right hand corner). Make sure to include the 10-digit ISBN number of the physical edition and the ASIN of the Kindle book.

The reality, I've had to call KDP support to get my print and eBook versions linked together almost every time.

**CREATESPACE TO KINDLE**

If you publish your paperback version first, you'll have the option of pushing your book from CreateSpace to Kindle.

**Note, this is not something we'd recommend, because the interior file for a paperback is vastly different from the Kindle version, so always opt to do these two things individually.**

When you publish your paperback version, you'll be

prompted to send the book to Kindle. Since we already published our book to KDP, simply opt out and provide the reason, "I already have a Kindle version."

## HTML DESCRIPTION STUFF FOR BOTH, WHAT KEY-WORDS TO PUT IN COPY

You can use the same description you used for your KDP version.

## IMAGES

If you're using images in your print version, these need to be at least 300 DPI. Anything less than that and your images will be grainy or blurry.

Here's the official CreateSpace blurb: *Images may be CMYK or RGB color. All images should be sized at 100%, flattened to one layer, and placed in your document at a minimum resolution of 300 DPI.*

# SETUP AND UPLOADING

**TITLE**

Once you have your CreateSpace account, click on "Add New Title."

You'll be asked to name your project. Typically this is the title of your book. Then choose the type of project it is; in this case, you're creating a paperback.

The next option you'll see is the type of setup. We'd recommend that you opt for the guided setup option. This provides you with everything you'll need and steps you through the process, whereas the other option doesn't provide you with as much access.

If you're unsure of the process, choose the guided option.

Enter the title or name of your book here.

**SUBTITLE**

If your book has a subtitle, enter it here. Your title and subtitle together must be fewer than 200 characters. The subtitle will appear on your book's detail page, and must adhere to the same guidelines as for your title.

**Remember to make this match your KDP version.**

Later, if we change the KDP title or subtitle, the books will remain linked. However, once you get an ISBN for your print book, the Title and Subtitles cannot be changed in CreateSpace.

## AUTHORED BY

Author, editor, foreword, illustrator, introduction, narrator, photographer, preface, translator.

 At least one author name is required.

You can add other contributors as needed.

## SERIES TITLE

You can choose if your book is part of a series. If so, you can enter a series title here. When you enter a series title, enter only the name of the series.

To ensure customers can find all the books in the series, do not add the individual book title or volume number in the series title field, and make sure you use the same series title for all the books in your series.

## EDITION NUMBER

A version is a particular edition of a book. Identifying the version number helps readers determine whether the book is the original edition, or if it contains updated content.

If this is the first time you've published this book, enter the number one (1). If the book was previously published and the version you are publishing contains significant changes, enter the number two (2) (and so on).

## PUBLICATION DATE

Your publication date is typically today's date, or if you've published the Kindle version already, you can choose that as your publication date.

**You cannot choose a date in the future, so you need to be ready to upload your book files at this stage.**

## ISBN

**You need an ISBN number to publish the print version.**

Here are your four options:

1. The free one assigned by CreateSpace.

2. $10 Custom CreateSpace-owned ISBN (you can use this only on CreateSpace).
3. $99 Custom Universal ISBN (that you can use anywhere).
2. Provide your own, previously purchased, ISBN (more expensive).

As soon as you've chosen an option and clicked on "save," the ISBN number is locked and cannot be changed.

This means that should you decide to change the title of your book, you'll have to create a new book with a new ISBN. And remember, you can't change the title of a paperback once the ISBN has been issued.

This is CreateSpace's verbose explanation of the ISBN options:
https://www.createspace.com/Products/Book/ISBNs.jsp

But this is the best independent explanation I've read:
http://www.sellbox.com/how-choose-isbn-options-using-createspace-print-demand-printer/

## PUBLISHER

Enter the publisher name that you would like listed for your book on the book's detail page. This can be an individual or company name.

Note that this option is only available if you've provided your own ISBN.

## INTERIOR

Once you reach the "interior" page, you'll need to make sure that the right book size is showing.

Most paperbacks are 5" x 8" (fiction) or 6" x 9" (non-fiction). Choose the option that you formatted your interior file with.

You'll also choose whether the interior text is black and white or color. (Most books will be black and white.) And also, choose what color the paper will be—white or cream.

Choose your options carefully. Most non-fiction books use white paper and most fiction internals are cream.

## UPLOAD YOUR BOOK FILE

This is where that hard work of compiling your .pdf file comes in. "Browse" for your book's .pdf file and upload it here.

Make sure that your text ends before the edge of the page—this is the bleed area. It's selected as default, but it pays to make sure that it's ticked.

Once you're ready, click "save" and then wait while CreateSpace processes your files.

**NOTE: This process can take 5-10 minutes; do *not* exit your browser while this is happening.**

After your file has finished uploading, you'll be told straight away if there are any issues with images or anything else. At this point, you should launch the interior reviewer to see what those issues are.

If you need to make changes, do it, recompile, and then come back and re-upload the new file.

If nothing needs changing, you can click "save and continue" or "ignore issues and continue," depending on what you're doing.

## UPLOAD YOUR COVER

Choose how your cover will look by opting for a matte or glossy finish. This is purely up to individual choice, no right or wrong option here. However, I've found that the glossy covers that are printed from CreateSpace look a little bit more professional.

### Upload Your Cover

And here comes that beautiful cover you had made. "Upload a print-ready PDF cover," find it, and upload it.

You have a couple of other options. Pay to engage CreateSpace's professional services or use their built-in cover builder. Ignore these. We do *not* use CreateSpace's cover builder . . . ever.

When you're ready, click "save" and wait for the cover to be uploaded. Again, this can take a while, so grab a coffee while you wait. . .

Once you've gotten to this point, your files will need to be submitted for review. If you're not quite ready to do that, then save and come back to your project at a later date.

If you are ready, click "submit files for review." This process will take 12-24 hours, and then you'll receive an email from CreateSpace prompting you to review and approve your files.

## PROOF YOUR BOOK

Once your book has been through the CreateSpace review process, you'll be able to proof your book.

You have two options to do that:

1. Digital proof
2. Physical proof

We'd recommend that you do both, particularly if this is the first time that you're doing a paperback. You want to make sure everything is where it's meant to be, that images look right, and that the cover looks how you want it to.

The physical proof can take a few days to get to you, so while that is happening, your book's unable to be published.

Once you're happy with the proof, click "approve" and move to the next step.

**CHANNELS**

Once you've proofed your book, you're ready to complete the remainder of the process.

If you've chosen to use the free CreateSpace assigned ISBN, you'll have access to all the sales distribution channel's listed.

If you've uploaded your own ISBN, some of the sales distribution channel's will not be available.

Choose all the channels that you can access. Then click

"save and continue."

## PRICING

On the pricing page, you have three marketplaces to list your price: USA, UK, and Europe.

By default, UK and Europe are ticked to adjust pricing based on whatever you enter in the USA box.

When deciding on your pricing, you'll note that just underneath the USA pricing box is a dollar amount. This is the minimum that you can sell your book for based on what it costs to produce and on CreateSpace's margin.

Most paperbacks are priced anywhere between $9.99-$23.99, but it's really up to you and the genre/niche of your book.

Your book, your decision. Hello, indie author!

Choose a figure, enter it in the USA pricing box, and then click "calculate." This will provide you with the commission amounts you'll get on the right hand side.

Click "save and continue" once you're done.

You'll be shown your cover again; click "save and continue" to move to the next step.

## DESCRIPTION

Like the copy on the inside flap of a hardcover book, the description tells readers a bit about your book. You can enter a description for your book that's between 30 and 4000 characters.

At this time, multimedia items such as embedded YouTube videos are not supported in the description.

**NOTE: The book description on your title's detail page may be delayed but should appear within 72 hours.** If you've already published the Kindle version, use the same description from there so that they match.

## BISAC

Here's where it gets interesting again.

Remember those two categories that we researched before? On CreateSpace, you can only choose one of them. Choose the main one that fits your book best.

Once again, CreateSpace categories may not match up, so you'll need to do a bit of digging until you can find the right one that's the closest.

## LANGUAGE

Amazon has a list of languages. English is the most common and it bears discussing other languages, but the bulk of current CreateSpace royalties are for English titles.

That being said, there are starving markets in Germany and Brazil that we know indie authors are translating their books into native languages for.

We'll get into new markets in another book.

## KEYWORDS

Probably the second most important selection on the list.

In CreateSpace, you can enter four to five keywords and there's a character limit for each keyword of 25 characters, so some of the long-tail keywords that you used in KDP may not fit.

## ADULT CONTENT

If your book contains adult content, and that's subjective, you'll want to click that box. But beware, this can only reduce the number of readers that Amazon will present your book to in searches, so be careful.

Then click "save and continue."

At this point, you'll be prompted to upload your book to Kindle. Since we already did that, skip this and you're done. Now you just have to wait for the proof to come back.

In the meantime, let's make sure people know who you are as an author.

# AMAZON AUTHOR CENTRAL

**WISK**

"Who are you?" — Steve Windsor

**SETTING UP YOUR AUTHOR CENTRAL ACCOUNT**

Your Author Central profile is how readers are going to get to know you on Amazon.

When someone clicks your author name next to your book's title, they'll be directed to your Amazon author page. It has things like a professional photo of you, your bio, your books, and information you want readers to know about you and your writing.

It's also where you can connect your blog and Twitter feed, and how you "claim" all of your books. Think of it as a dashboard for everything you've written and published on Amazon. Your reviews are in there, as are each of your books' sales rankings.

To set up your account, follow the steps outlined on Amazon's "Setting Up Your Author Central Account" page.

## CLAIMING YOUR BOOKS

Once your book is uploaded, you're approved it and it's available for sale. In theory, Amazon and CreateSpace should've assigned it to your Amazon Author Central Profile Page. However, I find that it's hit or miss for this to happen. So what you'll have to do is log in to your Amazon Author Central account, go to your "Books" tab and then click the "Add More Books" button.

Search for your missing book. If it hasn't been assigned to your profile yet, click the button that says "This is My Book," to add it to your Author Central Profile.

Now your book is published, available for sale, and attributed to you as an author.

# NEXT STEPS

Congratulations, you're "published."

I know all of that felt complicated and anything new always does. However, after you do it once, it gets infinitely easier.

If you've followed the steps in this book, your first book is now available on Kindle and/or CreateSpace.

We wrote this book because we wanted to share what we've learned from self-publishing our own stories.

By walking you through the process of compiling, uploading, and publishing your books, we hope that we've provided some useful insights and insider tips on getting your first book "right."

**The next step's up to you.**

Now it's time to fire up your marketing skills, and we are going to discuss that in the next *Nine Day Novel* installment on Book Marketing.

I encourage you to **follow my progress as an author and get access to awesome tools** and how-to guides to use on your own author journey.

To entice you, we wrote a free book for you, *29 Truths From the Trenches of Self-Publishing*.

You can get that book and get notified when our new authorship books come out, by clicking HERE. You can also visit http://authorbasics.com/lp1 and subscribe.

**You can reach me here:**
Email: steve@authorbasics.com

**Other author how-to books in the *Nine Day Novel* series:**

9 Day Novel: Authorphobia
9 Day Novel: Outlining
9 Day Novel: Writing
9 Day Novel: Self-Editing
9 Day Novel: Self-Publishing
9 Day Novel: Book Marketing -- coming in 2016
9 Day Novel: Writing a Series -- coming in 2016

# ABOUT THE AUTHORS

## STEVE WINDSOR

I'm just a guy who decided to write one day. And roughly two years and two million words into it, I've learned so much and my writing has improved so much. . . But it all came at a cost in time and frustration. I've bled words.

One of the things I related to an interviewer was that if you find the thing that will make you deny yourself sleep, food, bathroom breaks, even sex . . . then that's your calling. Mine is to write and help other authors overcome their fears and grow their writing "muscle."

I'm here to help you grow as an author. The best way you can do that: Go write something!

— Steve Windsor

## LISE CARTWRIGHT

I'm the gal who decided that working in the corporate grind was boring and that there had to be more to life. Four years later, job left and I have a full-time writer and author career . . . well in place!

I'm all about doing what you love, because life is short, who wants to spend their time doing stuff that sucks, or doesn't mean something to YOU? Figure out what you love to do then figure out how to turn it into moola; while helping people along the way—that's my life's mantra.

Stick with me, I won't lead you down the garden path. I'm in the trenches with you as an author and I want to see you succeed. But the only way that's gonna happen is if you get off your butt and take action!

— Lise Cartwright

# WE NEED YOUR HELP!

**Thank you for reading this book!**

We'd love to get your input so I can make the next book even better. We're not above bribing you with an Éclair.

Wasn't that tasty? All we ask in return is that you leave a constructive review by visiting https://authorbasics.com/ndn-self-publishing-review/

Thanks so much!
Steve & Lise

www.ingramcontent.com/pod-product-compliance
Lightning Source LLC
Chambersburg PA
CBHW071153290526
45787CB00001BA/332